AWAKEN *the* SILENCE
WHEN SILENCE ISN'T GOLDEN

VIVIONNE GRACE KELI

Author, Speaker and Survivor

VIVIONNE "GRACE" KELI

Author, Speaker and Survivor

Printed in the USA
Copyright © 2009 Vivionne Grace Keli

Contents of this book may not be reproduced electronically, copied whole or in part, translated or faxed to a machine-readable form without the written authorization of Vivionne G. Keli. Please contact info@holdyourpeace.com For Press Kits, CD's and Speaking Engagements please Write to:
Hold Your Peace Seminars
P.O. Box 177
La Verne, California 91750

Scriptures cited for this book have been taken from an electronic version of the King James Version (Crown copyright/Public Domain in the United States).

Scripture taken from the New King James Version. Copyright © 1982 by Thomas Nelson, Inc. Used by permission. All rights reserved.

The stories mentioned in this book are actual events from the author's past. Some names have been modified to protect the privacy of people involved.

All rights reserved.

ISBN: 1-4392-4978-4
ISBN-13: 9781439249789

Visit www.booksurge.com to order additional copies.

"Stolen innocence may never be regained or forgotten. It can only be viewed as a loss by force. Our real hope is to learn and break the cycle and when we do, then, our experiences will be wisdom and power to protect the innocence of others"

Keli 2020
Having the Vision

Preface

Dear Prospective Reader,

I pray that this book finds you in God's loving arms. If you are reading this book, you or someone you love may have experienced, or are experiencing, hurt. You are not alone. I ask that as you begin your journey toward recovery, you become honest with whom you are. Can you look at yourself in the mirror and say that you are a survivor, a victorious being, and a loved person?

Have people mistreated you in the past or maybe even now, and you cannot seem to be around them? Do you wish them ill or maybe death? Are you frustrated and depressed because of the way you feel toward the people who caused you great pain? Are you torn between your pain and your belief system? Are you tired of hypocritical Christians? Do you desire to come back home to God, but you do not know how? The only way you can come back home is to start with yourself; allow God into your life. You see, we all have a story, and only you have lived your story. However, you are not alone in your suffering.

As a Christian woman, I have taken the greatest challenge this world has to offer—to walk in faith and obedience to God. No matter how hard it seems, keep pressing on. Challenges will come and go. Remember, help is on the way. I once read a scribble on a library table that said, *"When you are going through troubles, hold on, keep holding on, and don't give up, just hold on."* There will be challenges in our lives, and how we handle them is crucial to our very existence on earth, but most importantly in heaven. We will experience many things; people will harm us physically, mentally, emotionally, and spiritually, but our faith must surpass them all.

"These things I have spoken unto you, that in me ye might have peace. In the world ye shall have tribulation: but be of good cheer; I have overcome the world." John 16:33 KJV

Your challenges are about to begin so say to the Lord, give me strengthen to climb this mountain Lord, for I am ready be to be transformed.

Love & Blessings,
Vivionne Grace Keli

Dedication

This book is dedicated to all those who have survived sexual abuse or any dehumanizing acts toward them or someone that they love. The key to spiritual healing is FORGIVENESS! Once you open up your heart to forgiving yourself and others, your life will experience a metamorphosis. Join me in my quest to eradicate such horrendous crimes towards children by educating others and awakening the silence.

This book is also dedicated to my beautiful, intelligent, and amazing daughters. Thank you both for forgiving me. To my husband, Sangman, thank you. A special thank you goes out to my spiritual sister and best friend, Marvell Bryant, for her patience, love, and understanding and her mother Jennie Hamilton for always having faith in me. Most importantly, I dedicate this book to God, who has allowed Pastor Mic and Jana Thurber, Pastor Carl Rodriguez and a sister in Christ Bruni Quiñónez for never giving up on me.

What a wonderful feeling it is to live in a country that women still have rights to be heard and seen.

God Bless America!

Acknowledgements

My life has been touched by many individuals and because of them I am alive, happy and blessed today.

Daughters, Brina and Ross you both are my beautiful, intelligent, and amazing daughters, thank you both for forgiving me and allowing me to be in your lives. I am looking forward to many years of happiness with you both and your families.

Sangman Lee, my loving and inspiring husband, thank you for teaching me patience and for having patience.

Marvell Bryant, you never gave up on me. Thank you for stopping me from committing suicide in 1997 and literally saving my life. You are my inspiration, my sister and my best friend. No one knows me like you do. Thank you for being in my life.

Jessica Bryant and little sisters, my youngest of inspirations, you are all awesome nieces and I am so glad to have you all in my life. Thank you for sharing your insights with me. Love Auntie Gracie.

Jennie Hamilton, thank you for always having faith in me. I also thank you for dropping everything and helping me on this project at the last minute. I love your laugh, your voice and your spirit. May God continue to bless you and your family.

Pastor Mic and Jana Thurber, you both were instrumental in my recovery process. I never forgot what you have told me as a teen. I pray that God will continue to use you both to reach other teens that are hurting.

Pastor Howard and Lisa Small, you both are so special to me and I love you both. Thank you for being part of this special project. I am looking forward to many more projects in the future.

Pastor Carl Rodriguez, thank you for taking heed to God's calling. You were the turning point that led me to choose the path to the cross. May God continue to inspire you and bless your ministry.

Bruni Quiñónez, my sister in Christ, thank you for allowing God to lead you into my life and being there on the day of my baptism. I love you with the love of our Lord and Savior Jesus Christ. May God continue to place you in the lives of the hurting so that they may see Him.

Jean Taylor, thank you for rescuing me and my daughters when we were at the verge of being homeless. I haven't really told you how much you, your mom and family mean to me. I love you. Thank you.

Japhena Musson, thank you for all your support and prayers. May God continue to bless you as a Life Coach and your endeavors as Communications Specialist.

Nichell Hurley, thank you for your encouragement and love. I am looking forward to reading your book soon.

My stepmother, thank you for encouraging me and being part of my past. Although at first our paths did not meet, I am thankful that we became excellent friends. You are an awesome woman and never forget that.

Dad, you are very special to me and I will always love you. Thank you for encouraging me in writing this book. Never forget how much you mean to me.

My sisters, I love you all I with all my heart. If it weren't for my sisters I do not know where I would be today. I thank you all!!!

Nesta Paul, I thank God for placing you in my life, thank you for being my spiritual mentor and a voice of reason.

In Loving Memory of
Alexandria Rachel Zepeda
1988 to 2009

TABLE OF CONTENTS

~Seasons of Pain

Chapter 1 3
A Thief Comes to Destroy

Chapter 2 11
The Beast And No Beauty

Chapter 3 25
Stolen Innocence

Chapter 4 33
The Day the Rainbow Ceased

Chapter 5 41
Will It Ever End?

Chapter 6 45
Massachusetts Here We Come!

Chapter 7 49
California Here We Come!

Chapter 8 57
Forgiven By My Molester?

~Time of Self-Actualization

Chapter 9 65
The Psych Ward, My Happy Home

Chapter 10 71
The Era of Errors

Chapter 11 81
A Chair Is Still a Chair

~The Journey to Finding "Grace"

Chapter 12 93
When Love Finds You

~The Road to Recovery

Chapter 13 101
Forgiveness Conquers All

Chapter 14 115
Finding The Treasure Within

Chapter 15 127
Finding Life On "Root 66"

Chapter 16 135
Becoming An Effective Warrior

Chapter 17 141
When God Feels Far Away

Chapter 18 147
Awaken The Silence

Chapter 19 151
God Cannot Do...

Chapter 20 161
Surrendering To Forgiveness

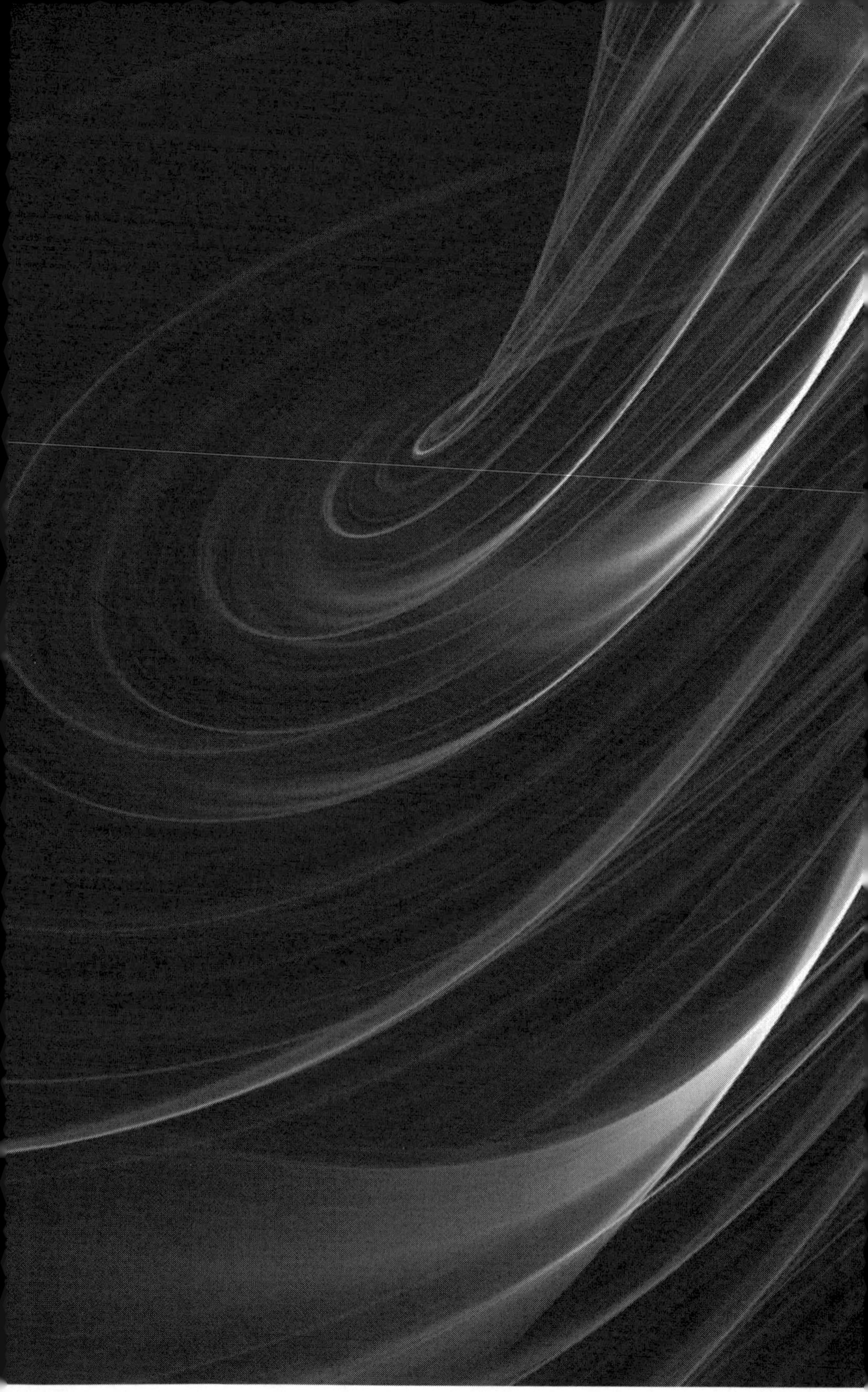

Seasons of Pain

Chapter 1

A Thief Comes to Destroy

"¹The thief cometh not, but for to steal, and to kill, and to destroy: I am come that they might have life, and that they might have it more abundantly." JOHN 10:10 KJV

I used to wonder why, as a child, I felt so angry, confused and bitter. Looking back I can attribute it to always wanting to be better, but instead I remained bitter. Who would teach me, and what did being better really mean? Often, I would ask myself…was I misplaced, and when did I lose control of my life? Am I the only one with a family who is totally insane? At a young age I realized, the people who raised me were mentally and emotionally unstable, not to mention they had a distorted view of Christianity, a view that ultimately changed my life.

As you read the following chapters, you may feel as though your situation pales in comparison to mine. But if you've experienced one molester, one rapist, or one assailant, one is too many. As you read this book particular scenarios may cause you to recall unpleasant memories from your past. Remember, they are from the past. I encourage you to make a conscious choice to remain in the present. Surround yourself with objects that are reminiscent of joyous occasions. Some examples might include pictures, the Bible, with its many promises, an inspiring book, or even write letters of love to yourself. These items can be used as positive triggers to evoke happier moments in your life. Also, find a Christian counselor, or a good friend you can trust and confide in. My best friend is Marvell whom I can call on any time, day or night and know, without question, that she will listen and understand. Joining a support group or a church organization can also be extremely beneficial. If your church does not have a support group, then start one by asking a women's ministry leader or your pastor to help you.

Contrary to popular belief of many renowned psychologists, I believe true healing occurs when you confront and analyze issues from the past. I'm not advocating that one should ruminate about their past. However, if you think you've tried everything, don't stop, but continue to look deeper and search for the catalyst to your dysfunction. Behavioral issues usually stem from your past. You can't change your past, but you can improve your future. Keep in mind that nothing changes overnight. It is a process.

In this chapter, *"A Thief Comes to Destroy,"* Who is the thief and what does he want? *"The thief cometh not, but for to steal, and to kill, and to destroy:"* [1] Now, let us dissect this verse step-by-step. This specific thief comes for us physically; however his evil works are mostly in the spiritual realm. The greatest disadvantage that humans experience is that we are battling against someone we can't see. The emotional blows to your body are devastating, and although unseen the blows are evident through our actions, thoughts and behaviors towards situations and people. This thief, I call him by his name, Satan, comes to steal, kill, and destroy you and me.

This has been his mission from the day of his fallout with Christ. Satan comes to steal. Nothing frustrates me more than someone stealing from me. Have you ever had a sentimental attachment to something, and had it taken from you without your consent? How did you feel; violated and angry? What does this thief want?

Satan lies in wait, ready to attack or minds when we are most vulnerable. The thief's prize possession is not only the physical, but also the mental, which leads to the soul. Stealing the mind is the first part, but what about the kill? Under control of the thief the mind begins to die; hence, the thief is killing the spirit, the mind, and the person completely. For example, a child decides to take his brother's goldfish... The goldfish is swimming in his natural environment, water, but then...swoop...the goldfish is now in this little boy's hand... What will happen if he keeps the fish out of water? Eventually, the goldfish will die, just as our minds will die if out of God's possession and in control of the Thief.

Destruction, of the mind, is not always instantaneous, but usually a very slow process. It's important for us to understand that Satan loves to entertain us with issues from our past. How important is the mind to Satan? If a person is in a severe car accident, loses total mobilization, and the body no longer functions, but there is no damage to the brain, and the mind continues to work, then is the person dead? No! The body may be inept, but the brain is still functioning. If the brain did not experience trauma the mind continues to perform. In this case, the patient has the ability to cognitively choose to accept what has happened and cope or not. Let's review another scenario; how about if the body is functioning, but there is no brain activity or function...would you consider the body lifeless or dead? What good is a brain that Satan cannot use? Satan would rather plague the mind of a person who lost mobilization by constantly reminding them of the days they used to walk and have fun. Satan seizes these opportunities to dishearten individuals.

Through my season of pain I concluded, the mind is a battlefield. So my question for you is...have you allowed Satan to imprison your mind? Who has planted the seeds of fear, self-hatred and mistrust within you? Let us also keep in mind that Satan not only uses his arsenal of weaponry, but enlists accomplices who carry out his evil plans.

I invite you to momentarily revisit the past. Who has Satan strategically placed in your childhood or in your adult life who've caused you pain, and in many cases spiritual death? Have you forgiven them? Probably not! I ask this question because unresolved issues, from your past, can take precedence over your life causing you to remain dormant in areas where growth is imperative for the survival of your mind. Today, will you begin the journey of releasing these individuals from your past? At times your pain may seem never-ending, but you must be willing to give up something. What? Your past! Trust me, I have been there. You must be willing to forgive those who've violated your trust, and in the process, learn to love yourself... Love and forgiveness are essential elements necessary for the healing process to begin.

If you are like what I once was, you may have never really known what it feels like to love or be loved. Unfortunately, survivors of abuse sometimes confuse the definition of love and the act of loving responsibly. What do I mean when I refer to responsibly? Some survivors have a tendency, to give too much of themselves. Then you have others who detach themselves by not loving enough. All throughout history it seems that many survivors were taught to love others and forget themselves completely. It's been my own personal experience that we must love ourselves. Please understand that I am not speaking about loving yourselves like the *"world"* states we should love ourselves.

Love suffers long and is kind; love does not envy; love does not parade itself, is not puffed up; does not behave rudely, does not seek its own, is not provoked, thinks no evil; does not rejoice in iniquity, but rejoices in the truth; bears all things, believes all things, hopes all things, endures all things. (1 Corinthians 13: 4-8) NKJV

How do you begin to love yourself, and understand what love really means? The answer is quite simple be kind to yourself and others. Respect yourself. Remove any negative thoughts of others and don't wish evil on them no matter how evil they are towards you. Be true, have hope, and become reacquainted with yourself and whatever you expect others to do for you, do it for yourself and others as well. Most importantly, get to know who God is and what He desires for you. Also, treat yourself with care by eating right, exercising, and getting adequate rest. In addition, it is important to journal and even more important to write or email love letters to yourself naming all the good qualities you possess; all the wonderful assets God has given you. Make a list of God's promises, on paper and in your heart. To view some of these promises, please look in the back of this book.

Because so many of you are accustomed to being surrounded by negativity, I realize the task of looking at yourself in the mirror and seeing who you are as well accepting every feature about you, let alone loving yourself, might be quite difficult. But remember, whatever you desire in a person, become that person yourself. If you desire love, love more (responsibly) [2], if you desire wisdom seek to be wise from the Bible [3]. If you desire to have an exciting person in your life, become an exciting person and when you are ready for that special someone to come into your life God will lead them to you. Allow God to mold you into who you were destined to be.

Find out how much God loves you [4], and read one of the most beautiful letters written in history-the Bible. God says *"For I know the thoughts that I think toward you, saith the LORD, thoughts of peace, and not of evil, to give you an expected end."* (Jeremiah 29:11) KJV

Remember, the battle is for your mind and there are two key players God and Satan. Satan will place every obstacle in your path to achieve his goal but God has the power to override any attacks on your mind and soul.

As I travel and speak, to diverse groups of women, I'm often asked how I overcame my childhood pain. Time after time, I respond to them by asking if they thought that I had a choice. I tell them, *"I made the choice to take back what belongs to me, and regain control of my life."* I then proceed telling these hurting women that we all have a choice, to accept life, cope, and move forward, or stay in the muck of the past and experience a slow death of mind, body and soul.

Several years ago I was asked, by an amazing, beautiful, and intelligent woman named Gina, *"How do you stop the hurt?"* My answer to her was, *"Do you want to stop the hurt or speak about stopping the hurt?"* She gave me a puzzled look as if to say, what are you getting at? I answered, *"What have you tried before that has not worked and what are you trying now?"* She replied, that she had been praying a great deal. I told her, *"Okay! Prayer is excellent, but do you believe in what you pray for? Do you pray for forgiveness of the person or individuals that hurt you?"* "Yes!" She replied. *"Have you set boundaries with the person who has caused you great pain?"* She responded, "No!" There was her answer. We need boundaries.

Just like real estate where you have *"metes and bounds, we must have metes and bounds,"* in place, to protect our mind, body and soul. We are God's property and He holds the deed which He achieved at the cross. As God's children, we must be responsible in protecting God's property, and anyone crossing those boundaries we have set for ourselves, is infringing on our personal property. Boundaries are a factor in the healing process. If you don't know your personal, mental and emotional boundaries, no one else will know them either. Gina needed to place a *"no trespassing"* sign that enabled others to know her boundaries so that she could *"hold her peace."*

When I say hold your peace [5], I mean keep the Giver of peace in your heart, but still speak your peace. With boundaries, you can love someone, but you do not have to like them, their actions, their behavior, or their attitudes. I told Gina that when she prayed, she must pray for those who hurt her, those who hate her, those she despises, and more importantly, pray for the strength to forgive them. It took Gina a long time to actually comprehend what I was saying, but now, with God's help, she is on the road to recovery.

We may never forget the past or those who caused us pain, but we cannot allow the past to dictate our future. Therefore, we must be rooted in the WORD of God; not only one book but all 66...books. Root 66, not the world famous Route 66 highway, but the BIBLE, The only way to know God is by truly knowing His word.

It takes time to heal, and from this day forward, you must be realistic, patient and hold yourself accountable to make a change. Are you ready?

Chapter 2

The Beast and No Beauty

"The unforgiving person is like the foolish man who says, give me poison that I may drink and avenge my enemies, for I will not forgive their trespasses against me and I will show them how wise I really am." —VIVIONNE "GRACE" KELI

My life's journey began in 1966, deep in the heart of the ghetto in the South Bronx. It was my father and mother's *"making of a fatal attraction."* Although, there wasn't physical fatality, fatalities were in the emotional, spiritual and mental sense. My parent's attraction was volatile and toxic and because of this, many members of my family, Aunt Rita Aunt Lisa, Uncle Dennis, Grandmother, who I call Mami and dad, raised me. I was constantly shuffled around like luggage and never really felt at home unless I was with Mami. The only people that I really attached myself to were with my uncle, aunts, Mami and dad. I loved Mami because she was the only one that loved me. I was Mami's little shadow and when she wasn't around I became anxious and could not function.

However, when I was at my biological mother's house, she constantly reminded us that she did not want us kids. Even now, it isn't easy for me to know that children are not loved from conception. The hardest part is when a child knows that they were used to entrap another human being. Love was never the motive for having my sister Yvonne and me. We were merely pawns in a one-sided game.

Let me introduce you to my parents. Dad, in his day, was known as a *"ladies' man."* He was suave, sleek and extremely handsome. Dad always made an entrance. Yes, dad knew how to strut his stuff; yet, in a humble way. He was also a gentleman, in fact, married and single women would confide in him, and divulge their inner most secrets. He never made enemies with other men because men knew that dad was honorable. My father was the man! He was the youngest of three. Dad never knew his father because he was killed in an automobile accident when he was only a few weeks old. Dad's life was not easy from childhood and there were many variations to his upbringing, but what seemed to be the common theme was that Mami left Puerto Rico when dad was very young to go and make a life in New York City. Her plan was to send for the kids when she became settled. Unfortunately, Mami became deathly ill with pleurisy and did not have much luck, so when she did settle down dad was much older. It was not until dad was about sixteen years of age that he finally went to live with Mami and her new husband Rosendo.

The progenitor which I call *"mother"*, she was a true beauty. Sometimes, I would sit and gaze at her because I thought she was the most beautiful woman in the world. She could walk down the street and men would stop in their tracks to give her a compliment, whistle or blow her a kiss. Mother's skin was pale like that of a porcelain doll with dark hair. Her hair was never out of place. She was thin but not the modern day thin, she had nice curves and knew how to wear her clothes. The rare times that I could actually get close to mother, I would observe her hands; they were always manicured and perfect. I remember telling other kids that mother was a movie star. But then, she would open her mouth, and pure evil would emerge.

Mother could make a sailor blush. Mother was the beast with no beauty in her. She could curse you out in Spanish and in English in a single breath and still maintain her composure. She did not care if she was coming out of church with a Bible in her hand. If you were a man and spoke to her and she did not like you, she was capable of beating you up physically with her Bible or cutting you up in the blink of an eye. She had the best uppercut I have ever seen. Dad can attest to that. Dad has always stated, *"I never received a punch by any man like the time your mother punched me in the eye, I don't know what she used but I was in pain for weeks."* He called that punch a satanic punch. He still laughs about it today.

In fact, if I had to describe mother, I would use three different movie characters. Mother had a little bit of Sally Fields, 1976 character of Sybil with her many personalities, Glen Close, 1987 classic character, Anne Archer the psychotic lover in Fatal Attraction, and Faye Dunaway's, 1981 role of Joan Crawford the excellent portrayal of an obsessive mother in Mommie Dearest. This summarizes my mother. The unfortunate part was that these characters were real for both my older sister Yvonne and me. You never knew which character would emerge. One tone in her voice could activate the sensors throughout our bodies alerting us that someone was coming out and it wasn't going to be pretty.

Personally, I believe that mother developed several issues when she was a child. The story that I have been told was that mother was born into an inter-racial couple. Her mother named Tita was a black Puerto Rican and her dad was a white Puerto Rican. I still don't know how the inter-racial card played here but, oh well. I guess it was more about color than anything else. Basically, it was the old standard, white versus black regardless of the fact they were from the same culture. Needless to say, mother hated her biological mother, Tita, to the point that she would deny her. Sometimes, Tita would attempt to pick mother up from school and mother would tell her classmates that she did not know who *"that black woman was."*

On the other hand, mother loved her father. Possibly because he was white however, I am going on my own speculation. No one will ever really know and it does not really matter. All I know is that for mother color meant a great deal. I simply do not understand how it is that mother had issues with color when three of her husband's were black, two Puerto Ricans and one Dominican. In truth, I believe that my mother hated Tita because she left my mom and her siblings behind in Puerto Rico when they were younger. Same story as my dad, a mother had to leave her children behind to make a life for her, and then send for the family.

Back then, Puerto Rico was going through some tough economic times and almost everyone traveled to the United States in search of a better way of life. Both my grandmother's were no exception. Grandmother Tita went to New York City with the promise of sending for her children. Unfortunately, while my mother was in Puerto Rico and being taken care of by a friend of the family, she was supposedly, molested by the friend's son, living in the home, at the time. Maybe this is why mother became so angry and hateful, or maybe it was guilt as an adult. You see, mother made some poor choices in her lifetime. For example, prior to meeting my father, mother broke up someone's marriage then became pregnant by this man. She forced him to leave his wife and marry her, and he did…but only after Yvonne was born.

The saga continues…mother got pregnant again but this time by my father while still married to Yvonne's father. Oops! I would think that would make someone live with great regret. Mother does not know if I am Yvonne's father's illegitimate daughter or Ben's whom I have called dad all my life. What an awful guilt to live with. This is why I strongly believe that sometimes extreme guilt is the reason that people hide behind religion, to cover their past sins.

I think this is why she attempts to play the role of a *"pious woman."* She is trying to hide something that she really isn't.

Nonetheless, the story must go on, because I could try to attempt to figure out why mother is the way she is, but that would be another book in itself, dealing with abnormal psychology. Whatever the reason, the bottom line is that mother had deep seeded hate and anger issues. Her hate manipulated her actions and ultimately her life and her children's lives as well.

In addition to mother's deep rooted issues, mother was known to be a very jealous woman, but not your typical low self-esteem jealousy; her jealousy was lethal. In her attempts to control my father, mother would make bomb threats to the church that my father attended. She stalked dad; she stalked Mami, she even stalked other women. Several times, she tried to kill dad with a butcher knife or a pair of scissors. On several occasions, my mother hired men to beat up on my father; thank God they never succeeded. Yet, he continued to go back to her.

When dad was with us, things got bad at home, dad had to escape and once again find refuge in Mami's house. It was while dad was staying with Mami that dad received a call that ultimately changed his life. Dad recalls the day he found out that I was born. It was June 28, 1966, when Mami received a call for my father. My father answered and a nurse, from Lincoln Hospital, told him that he needed to go to the hospital to fill out his daughter's birth certificate. He was shocked and so was Mami. They immediately headed out to the hospital where they found a little bundle of joy.

It was love at first sight, so my father says. Mami held me and they were very excited about my arrival! It was not long before my father moved back in with mother and they lived happily ever after...NOT!

It took two more years and my mother's persistence to make my father marry her. Of course she had to get a divorce from Yvonne's father first. Believe it or not, Yvonne's father was happy to accept her request because he was finally free from her. Dad, in his desperation, thought of a bright idea to avoid marrying mother. He told mother that he could not marry her because she was not of the same faith. As if that really mattered. Well, mother was not at all dumb, she found a very naïve pastor that would give her several quick Bible classes and she was ready for baptism in no time. Now, my father had to marry this *"damsel in distress."* I was already four years old, and mother was carrying yet another child. Dad was trapped and so, he married her. Not only was mother, now, a new Christian, and a married woman, but she remained in her other extra activities. Mother also practiced Santeria, a voodoo based religion.

Happiness eluded us and when both dad and mother were in the same room; mother abused him physically, emotionally and verbally. Unfortunately, we were subjected to watch in horror. Life was not easy for almost everyone in the home except the newest addition to our little family, my little sister Rachel. In my mother's eyes, my older sister Yvonne and I were considered, *"bastard daughters"* and that is how she raised us. Rachel was born after mother was married so she was the chosen child. The chosen one...

It so happens that on top of hating the entire universe, mother loathed Yvonne's father even after he met all her needs. Anything affiliated with her former husband, she hated. Therefore, she hated Yvonne and since mother did not know who my biological father was; she assumed that I was Yvonne's father's daughter. Mother has only loved one man and that is dad, therefore, she only acknowledges my baby sister Rachel. Insanity! To mother, it does not matter that Yvonne and I once shared the same womb as Rachel did. Mother openly admits it to anyone, that she only has one child regardless if we are present or not, and that child is non other than Rachel. Complicated? Yes, I know.

Mother played some sick games, which I was a part of. For instance, she would call Yvonne's father and make statements like, *"how do you feel that your daughter is being raised by another man?"* Then she would ask Ben, the man that I was being raised by, *"How do you feel that you are raising someone else's daughter?"* If you notice, she never acknowledges that I might be Ben's daughter. Fortunately, dad never paid any attention. I must admit, I have had my doubts that dad was my biological father because he was kind of an alien to me at times, especially when I was a teenager. But tell me, what teenager does not think that about their parents? Mother knew that Ben loved me with all his heart and what better way to hurt him?

Mother thrived on controlling my father and when she could not, she would abuse me to get back at him. There were many times that she attempted to take my life. Some incidents I can remember as if it were yesterday. Mother had us kids so that she could manipulate the men in her life and so when Yvonne's father or my dad was not around, mother neglected us. Often times, we were not bathed, didn't brush our teeth, weren't, fed or groomed and if we were lucky, we would have clothes on, other than panties and a camisole. In fact, we slept on a mattress without sheets for as long as I can remember.

When mother's evil sadistic side came out, I would spend days under the bed, so that mother would not abuse me. Anything could trigger her sadism and no one was safe when that happened. There was never a mother-daughter interaction unless she was beating or yelling at us. Mother did not hide how she really felt about my older sister, Yvonne or me, and she did not care if we heard it from her or anyone else. She hated us and that was the bottom line.

Actually, several witnesses have told me that on one occasion my mother placed a curse on me in public. Mother was going through one of her jealousy episodes. It happened that mother had a confrontation with a woman she suspected of having an affair with my father. While arguing with this woman, in church, the woman suggested that mother should be careful about what she says around me. Of course, mother was yelling and screaming outside the church so there was a large crowd of church members listening in. What came out of mother's mouth about me was shocking to everyone. Mother stated *"I hope Grace gets pregnant without getting married; I hope that she is sexually abused, and I hope she has men break her heart."* Everyone gasped at what she was saying. *"How could a mother curse her own daughter?"*

It goes without saying that mother hated me with a great passion and because of this, my father had great concerns for my life but yet, I remained in her possession. It got so bad that one day, my father followed mother and luckily he did, because mother decided to leave me in Central Park abandoned but dad picked me up and took me home. She was not even surprised that he found me. It was all a big sick game to her. I believe she knew that my father was following her. As a matter of fact, it was not unusual for mother to place me in precarious situations that I could have gotten hurt or even killed.

Once she threw me down a flight of marble stairs as we were leaving Mami's house. Mami told mother that she was an abuser and mother took me and left abruptly and although it may sound incredulous, I remember mother pushing me down a flight of stairs and as I was falling I remember being lifted up as if I were floating to the bottom of the stairs and seeing the tip of what looked like an Angel behind me. I can still feel the breeze that passed through my body. I looked up at mother, as to what had just happened. Mother looked amazed and became extremely angry that I did not get hurt. As I look back, if I had fallen head first down the flight of marble stairs I would be dead or incapacitated for life. What saved my life? Let's say, that I was a very blessed child to have possibly seen the direct work of a guardian angels.

Regrettably, it would seem to anyone that believes in superstition or curses that one of mother's curses came true because at age five, the church deacon, called Marty, but best known as *"the candy man,"* began to molest me. The *"candy man"* would carry a briefcase packed with all sorts of chocolate candies to lure his prey. No one could ever imagine that Marty was a molester because of his gentle disposition. Everyone thought that he was an innocent young man or had pity for him because when Marty was about five or six years of age Marty was struck by a vehicle while playing on the streets leaving him slightly physically impaired. However, Marty was extremely intelligent, but was terribly unattractive to the young ladies in church so he took a liking towards little girls.

Sadly, throughout the years, I learned that Marty also molested our neighbor's daughter Jane, she was fourteen years old, deaf and mute. She was also my babysitter, which would explain why Jane began to molest me as well. Jane and Marty molested me from age five to around age seven.

It was during this crucial time in my life that mother made me take on the role of an unwilling accomplice. It was my responsibility to report anything that I was exposed to when I would visit dad. Also, either Yvonne or I would have to accompany mother wherever she followed dad. We were taught not to be seen or heard and to keep a certain distance away or else we would be in big trouble. It seemed mother had an army of spies everywhere. . She also had powerful supernatural help. Mother would consult her spiritual guides to show her where dad would be physically or with whom he was seeing, and sure enough the voices in her head told her what she wanted to hear.

Dad could not understand how mother knew exactly where to find him because he would not tell anyone. He made every effort to conduct business and shop away from the Bronx by going to Manhattan, New Jersey, Brooklyn, Queens and even Long Island and low-and behold mother would find him. Just think, New York is not a small place and yet most often than not she managed to find him.

Some nights she would stay up creating incantations that were not at all favorable to my senses. She used roots and things for mixing up her concoctions of sorts and achieving amazing results. Unfortunately, mother also had spies that lived not too far from Mami's house. As soon as someone came to visit Mami's home one of her spies would call mother and she would go on a stake-out, often leaving us all alone, especially at night.

Yvonne and I knew that in addition to stalking, mother perfected unique investigative techniques. For as long as I could remember, while Yvonne was in school, and Rachel was being watched by either a friend or Tita, mother would take me, a seven year old, to the corner store located right on Prospect Avenue, a couple of blocks from the number five train and it wasn't to shop but to spy.

Mother became aware that the people she and dad knew would take their pictures to be developed at the Five & Dime corner store. Mother would methodically look through every name she recognized and opened their envelopes to look through everyone's pictures to see if she could find evidence that dad is being unfaithful. Unfortunately, in those days, pictures were not as secure as they are today. One specific day, mother hit the jackpot when she found one incriminating picture of my dad leaning over and talking to a young lady (I can still remember what was in the picture).

Mother questioned me about the young lady in the picture to see if I knew her or not. She asked me if I have ever seen this young lady visit Mami's house, and I said no. Apparently, mother thought that this picture must have been taken at Mami's house when dad was staying there. Mother had all the ammo that she needed to prove his unfaithfulness.

Finding this picture was the straw that broke the camel's back. She asked me again, *"Do you know who this girl is?"* and again, I said no. *"Do you see lots of girls going to your grandmother's house?"* I said yes (I did not know any better). All I knew was that Mami's house was a place that everyone went to after church to have meals, sing and fellowship. Then she said, *"Don't tell your father about this picture, I will speak to him later. You will do what I tell you when I need you."* This took place around the middle of the week and all was real quiet.

The following Sunday, dad was scheduled to pick me up, and my mother made sure that I was bathed, fed, and dressed. Once I was prepared, mother then told me what I was to do for her. I was to sit down on the couch, facing the door, and I was to ask dad to enter. That was all I thought at the time. Simple!

The scene was propped and the hour was at hand; when suddenly I heard footsteps coming up the marble staircase and then there was a knock at the door. Everything was going well. I was sitting in place, except that there was an added part to the equation that I was not aware of. Mother had a butcher knife in her hand and as I looked at her and she gave me a look of evil (one of her evil characters was about to emerge). My heart pounded, my stomach sank into my knees, and my nerves were uncontrollable, but with a soft, yet shaky voice, I told dad to come in. The doorknob turned and with each second my heart raced. I looked at mother, and she glared at me with pure evil. The doorknob finally clicked and my father opened the door. Every fiber of my being wanted to tell him to run but I could not.

He looked at me, but I could not move or say anything else. He must have seen the look of panic on my face. Dad then realized that I was looking at something behind the door. He jumped to the right, away from the door, when, the door slammed. Mother jumped at my father with the butcher knife. They fell to the ground and began to roll around. I could not move. My heart was pounding so hard I could hear it in my ears.

Mother was like a screaming banshee. Dad was trying to get her off of him but she had the strength of several men put together.

The struggle for the butcher knife seemed like an eternity. In the peak of the struggle, dad realized that I was sitting in my place and watching all of this. He yelled for me to leave the room, but mother wanted me to stay and watch. I listened to dad and I ran to another room and covered my ears. Afterwards, what appeared to take forever ended, and silence entered the room. I went to the living room to find dad, but he was gone. Mother was a mess; this was the first time I ever saw her in such disarray. I had failed her and now she was angry with me, so I ran under the bed where she could not get a hold of me. Afterwards, mother did not say anything to Yvonne or to me, about what had happened with dad. I was thinking that maybe he might be hurt. Did she kill him? Is he alright? I did not know what to think but I knew that he had to come back and get me.

Several days after mother attacked dad she called a truce. She decided to make dad a nice dinner, a Puerto Rican dish made with plantain called *"Pasteles"* and rice. Mother stayed in the kitchen, all day, cooking. Unfortunately, the only time that we saw mother cooking fancy meals were when men were coming over. Yvonne and I watched our mother cook, as little girls often do. We had an excellent idea! Why don't we cook like mother? So, we took some plantain peels from the trash and a can of white paint that we found in the closet and attempted to cook like our mother. We took the paint and mixed it up with the plantain, which made a big mess on the hardwood floors. We did not know any better, we were having fun. Mother was busy preparing her meal so she did not notice what we were doing. Dinner was complete and she waited, minutes turned into hours and my father never showed up.

Mother nurtured her seed of anger poisoning her soul. Blind furry overcame her and finally, after waiting and waiting, mother put all of the food away and came into our room. She was livid because of the mess we had created; compounded with her feelings of rejection from dad, she demanded that we undress ourselves and kneel in front of her with our faces toward the floor. Mother took a long black telephone cord and proceeded to whip us. She had no mercy. She was mad and angry with my father and she took her frustrations out on us; she kept on whipping us and whipping us. Our little bodies jerked with each blow as we squirmed on the floor. I lost control of my bladder, because the pain was excruciating, but that did not stop mother; she just continued. From head to toe, Yvonne and I had deep gashes from the beating. My skin was raw. When she finished, she had Yvonne wash me as she had always done in the past. I was in great pain, and my body was in shock. That night, Yvonne and I did not utter any words, we just whimpered ourselves to sleep. I slept under the bed so that mother could not hurt me again.

The following weekend, dad called to inform mother that he would be picking me up late in the afternoon. As usual, she prepared me to look like a little doll and acted as if nothing happened. When I saw dad, I was relieved that she did not kill him. Dad was happy to see me and off to Mami's house we went. Once we got to Mami's house, dad decided to get me ready for bed, and as usual, he ran the bathtub so I could take a bath. As he was taking my clothing off, he noticed the deep gashes on my legs, arms, between my thighs, and on the back of my head; he gasped and called Mami into the restroom. When she looked, she was beside herself.

The family was in an uproar and dad, for the first time in his life, took a stand and did something totally out of character. He abducted me. Within a couple of weeks, together with Mami, we arrived at the airport. However, upon our arrival, we experienced a little difficulty because I was not allowed to leave the United States without mother's consent. Dad was concerned because he knew that if I were to return to mother she would kill me. I remember sitting on a hard orange chair, swinging my feet back and forth listening to the heated conversation between dad, Mami and the airline representative. The airline representative was explaining the procedures when dad stated, *"If my daughter goes back to her mother she will kill her. Take a look at what she has done to my daughter."* Dad then proceeded to lift my dress to show the airline representative my scars. The man took a deep breath then he asked me who did this to me and I told him the truth, I answered *"mother."* He made his decision on the spot. He could not believe the abuse that I endured. We were soon off to Puerto Rico and leaving my dad, Yvonne and Rachel behind, never to see mother again. That was the last time that Yvonne and I played together as children or seen each other.

My first experience in Puerto Rico was a culture shock for me. However, I knew that a new dawn began and although I missed my father, I saw life for the first time full of colors and wonders. Puerto Rico was vibrant with many colors that I had never seen in my young life, all types of blue flowers, yellow flowers, white flowers and it was green with plenty of trees unlike the cement jungle that I was so accustomed to in the Bronx. The air was fresh. For some reason, I felt at peace. Even in my young age I had a sense of what peace could possibly be like. It was Mami and me living in a two-bedroom cottage that was owned by a friend of the family. Family came, and I got to meet more people than I could remember. I constantly missed dad and siblings. But in time, I learned to adjust, and was at peace. Arguments, physical abuse and emotional abuse were far from me and I was finally a little girl.

Chapter 3

Stolen Innocence

"Stolen innocence may never be regained or forgotten. It can only be viewed as a loss by force. Our real hope is to learn and break the cycle and when we do, then, our experiences will be wisdom and power to protect the innocence of others."

—VIVIONNE "GRACE" KELI

Sometime after Mami and I got settled in our little home, we received word that my favorite aunt Rita was relocating to Puerto Rico with her family. Rita was the younger of the two aunts, she was beautiful, intelligent and she knew it. Rita had boyfriends left and right and could never decide which one she like best. In fact, many church members did not want their daughters to be associated with my aunt Rita for her *"free spirit thinking."* Anyone that knew my aunt Rita knew that she was a very promiscuous young lady. Hence, she had gotten pregnant with Edward, a neighbor's brother and immediately began to have kids. Regardless what people thought of my aunt Rita, she was still my favorite aunt of the two. Knowing that she was coming to Puerto Rico made me extremely happy. I was excited because my cousins Catherine, Edward Jr. and Danny were also coming. I treated them as my siblings. We were raised together in Mami's house in New York City and being the oldest, I made it my responsibility to watch over them. I was so excited because that summer, I was turning eight years old and we were going to celebrate my birthday with my cousins, new friends and in a new place. It was the happiest and best birthday I ever had. Not too long after my birthday, Mami received a call, it was my step grandfather Rosendo. He had a little accident and Mami had to fly back to New York City to take care of him. I remained behind with my favorite aunt, Rita, and her family. Everything was going well, but financially my aunt was hurting because her husband could not keep a job. I do not recall how many months passed when I began to hear my aunt complain that my father was not sending money to take care of me. Contention between Rita and her husband, Edward, became common and, once again, I was in a very hostile environment.

Edward became a stay-at-home dad since he could not maintain a job. He took care of my cousins and on occasion he would take care of me when there wasn't enough bus fare for both my aunt and me to travel to school and the University together. Rita took a teaching position deep in the countryside, however, the University that she attended was in the opposite direction. On the days that she had to teach, and then attend the university, it would cost more, so, she would leave me with Edward.

One morning, Rita decided that she didn't have enough funds for us to travel so she left me behind with Edward. After Rita left to go to school, Edward came into the room, grabbed me by my hand, and took me to his bedroom. He lowered his pants and underwear and told me to do some vile things to him (without getting into specifics, Edward had me perform oral sex on him). After he released himself, I cleaned up and went to my room. I did not know what had happened, I was confused and I did not know what to do.

Within the same week, I began to wet the bed and Rita would get enraged. In the meantime, Edward could not leave me alone. Once I was sitting on the bed with my cousin, watching my aunt do something with her hair and Edward sat right next to me. He placed a pillow over my legs, and maneuvered his hands under the pillow and began to shove his finger up my private area; the pain was agonizing, and I never said a thing because of fear. He was making believe that he was resting his head on the pillow, with his arms under the pillow holding him up. Right in front of my aunt, he was hurting me, and I could not say a thing.

Bedwetting became more serious and my aunt became more hostile toward me. Rita did not have a washing machine and they were not as readily available as they are today. Rita had to wash the sheets that I messed up and she did not have any time or money for extra washes. I was an inconvenience. How could my favorite aunt treat me like this? I did not understand why she hated me so much. I could not comprehend what was going on, for this was the aunt who, when I was a baby, carried me everywhere. I thought she loved me. Now, she acted as if I were a nuisance. When I would wet the bed, she would ask Edward to discipline me and he did not hesitate. He would hit me with his thick plastic sandals. I would hide in the closet, but he would find me and he would hit and hit; it did not matter where the sandal landed.

My innocence was already compromised because of Edwards heavy petting, grooming and physical abuse. However, nothing prepared me for the day that Edward raped me. He came into my room as he had in the past and took me into his room. This time, however, it was different. He was very aroused, he took off all my clothes, made me lie on my stomach and then he raped me. I felt severe pain and thought I would die. I could not scream or move and felt helpless. I remember that my breathing was becoming faint because of his weight. My breath was slowly leaving my little body, my lungs were closing up and I felt like I was going away to another place. I kept praying for Edward to stop but he kept on. There was no angel to help me this time.

I remember turning my neck and looking at the red and white patterns, what looked like shields, on the wall. I remember little things, like the bed was not made and sound of the cartoons on the television. Once he finished, Edward told me to get up and put my clothes on. I did not understand anything of what was going on but more unsettling to me was Edward's treatment of me. He treated me with disgust. Edward told me, *"If you do not do what I tell you, I will tell your aunt of what you did."*

I felt confused. What did I do? After that, he attempted to get me or see me naked by walking into the bathroom while I was taking a shower. He made lewd comments about my private parts as if I was his prized possession. The more he would abuse me sexually, the more I would wet the bed. The more I wet the bed, the more he abused me physically and the less I ate. You see, not only did I receive my discipline physically, I was also denied eating as a source of punishment.

I confided in my friend, from next door, that Edward was doing bad things to me and that I was hurting and to be careful when she is around him. Unknowingly, my friend told her mother and her mother told Rita. I believe that Rita asked Edward but nothing became of it. All I can remember is that I lost a friend and Rita became very indifferent with me.

There was disdain in Rita's voice, especially when she spoke about my father not sending enough money. Yet, there was enough money for her kids because from out of nowhere they would get new clothes and shoes. Throughout my stay in Puerto Rico, I endured more abuse which left me sad and broken. Withdrawing from everyone helped me to cope. I believed that if they couldn't see me, they couldn't hurt me.

Finally, the day came when we heard from the States that my father was going to be married to a woman with two kids. She sent a big doll, specifically for me. The doll made an impact but just knowing that I was leaving made me excited! It was a bittersweet feeling for me because on one hand, I desired to leave Aunt Rita but on the other hand, I was going to miss my cousins. On the other hand, what a great time it was for me because, when word came, my uncle ceased from touching me again. The time came to pack up my meager belongings and move back to my father where I knew that I would be protected. As I was leaving, I had to give my big doll to my little cousin against my wishes. In a way, it did not matter to me because I was going back home to my dad, Mami and my own things, so I did not care.

Upon my arrival in the States, I was greeted by dad and others at the airport. I remember one person that was there whom I had a love-hate relationship with and that was, *"the candy man"* Marty. However, he did not matter to me, because I was back at home with my dad. We arrived at dad's new apartment and I walked through the door to find dad's wife, Nelda, who greeted me, kindly. Also, there was her daughter, Lily, and her son, Sammy.

As I settled in the apartment, I felt tension from my siblings. Apparently, before I arrived, the kids were misbehaving because Nelda kept threatening to spank them if they continued with their behavior. She kept warning them of the talk that they had prior to my arrival, but they continued. After dinner, the kids began to argue and she took them to the room and spanked them both. Soon after, Nelda returned from the room, she looked at me and then said the wrong thing, *"If you behave the same, I will hit you too."* My knees began to wobble and I began to panic. Is she going to abuse me too? Great, what should I look forward to now?

Time for bed quickly arrived. As we kids prepared ourselves to retire for the evening, Nelda's siblings came to visit one after the other to greet me. It was confusing because Nelda came from a family of eleven kids, eight from Nelda's mother's second marriage and two from Nelda's first marriage. This night, most of Nelda's half biological siblings came to visit me, honestly, I could not keep track. They all seemed to look alike. Several days passed, and we, as a family, had to visit Nelda's parent's home to introduce me. They lived not too far from our apartment so we could walk, but we took a taxi. I walked in the house to find a new step grandmother, Dolores, and step grandfather, Jose. I thought I could get used to them until, from out of nowhere, Jose said to me to, *"Get out of here you demon."* It was as if mother's demons invaded Jose. I thought, what, again? Within minutes, we were out of their home. No one said, I am sorry for his behavior, or please forgive us we won't take you there again. This left me thinking, is everyone sick? Why did Jose hate my father and me? Once again, it was because of racial tension and although everyone was Puerto Rican, apparently my father was not white enough to be accepted. Even one of Nelda's sisters made a comment that I looked like a Nigger and that I had Nigger hair, butt and lips. I did not understand what she was trying to say to me. What is a Nigger? Why would she call me this to my face?

As far as Nelda's parent's home, I would like to say that, this was the last of Jose, but for some reason Nelda had to go visit these sick people time after time regardless of how they treated me. Well, this all happened within the first week after arriving back from Puerto Rico. I was now officially a nervous wreck.

Panic set in when I realized how spoiled my newest siblings were, and what would be my issues with them in the future. As I look back, I was a great kid even with all the bad things that happened to me, I was trying to make everyone happy so that I would not have to be sent away from my father again. These new issues did bother me but the thought of being with dad made me feel a lot better. I was looking forward to seeing Mami for the first time in what seemed like infinity. Aside from all the past and new events in my life, it was nice to know that I was home again. And although I was not the same, I desired to be happy regardless of my circumstances. I did arrive to a grim reality that this was home; take it or leave it and make the best of it.

Chapter 4

The Day the Rainbows Ceased

"He who angers you, conquers you." —ELIZABETH KENNEDY

After being with my new family for a short time, we went to visit Mami's house. I ran up the flights of marble stairs and five floors, I was gasping for air, I reached the door. Oh how I missed Mami, for I knew she was the only one that truly loved me. It was nice to come home again. The home where I learned to walk, run and play hide and seek. This is where I shared many great Christmases, birthdays, many happy and not so happy occasions. Finally, Mami opened the door and I was home at last. I loved her so much and with a hug and a squeeze, I let go and ran straight to my room to find my belongings. I wanted to make believe that it was all a bad dream and finding something that was mine would help me wake up. I knew exactly where I had left my toys and things but they had been given away. I tried to find a little piece of my past, but to no avail. All I found was a Shirley Temple doll that I had received for Christmas prior to leaving the States. I hated that doll but she was the only thing left from my past.

How could they give away my toys?

After, I somewhat got over the fact that my belongings were given away, I settled with the Shirley Temple doll. All the same, I stayed with Mami for several days, to reacquaint myself and catch up on all the news. It felt nice to be with Mami and not worry about the *"new siblings"* interfering in my conversations. In a short period of time they managed to get on my last nerves. Everything looked the same but something was missing and I could not place my finger on it. Another thing that was quite different was that I was not emotionally the same. I knew that I was different spiritually, emotionally, and physically. I was pretty perceptive for my age. I was about to turn nine years old that summer but I felt much older, a little bit wiser and alert.

Safety was constantly on my mind and I would often ask myself if someone else would be hurting me again? I lived in fear and uncertainty because of my stepmother and her family and what they may do to me in the future. As I look back, I realize that there are days that I can remember incidents or events as if they just happened yesterday; they've been imprinted in my mind forever even while writing this book. There have been many events in my young life that have left an impact on me and Mami's visit this time wasn't any different. This visit ultimately changed my perspective on life completely.

Let me tell you how Mami's house impacted my life by giving you a brief history of *"the house."* Mami's house was unique in a strange kind of way. It was a refuge for most that visited, but there was a dark side to this house. Depending on what room one would visit, at the time, it could affect you a great deal. Everyone that visited Mami's house knew that her house always had guests from the physical and spiritual realm. This is the home where I was introduced to spirits. This is also the same place that I had my first encounter with the angel, when mother pushed me down a flight of marble stairs.

In fact, most of the spiritual guests were malignant entities, levitating people off their bed, with bodiless hands resting next to them. Spirits would materialize and dematerialize in front of people. These spirits tormented some members of my family, especially my aunt Lisa, Mami and me. As a child I felt that someone was always watching me and it was terrifying. On the other hand, I found comfort in some of the rooms.

I remember, on one occasion, grandmother Tita came to visit Mami. This was a rare occasion because they did not really interact with each other because Mami is a Christian and Tita was a Santera. I desired to see grandmother Tita, but as I began to walk toward the living room, where she was, a sudden strong wind came in from the window facing the east side of the house. Mami asked me to go close the window and as I began to walk away from the living room and down the long stretched hallway, I became stuck in the middle of the hallway, where to the left of me, was and imprint of a skeleton looking directly into the middle room. This room was where people would levitate off their bed or be caressed by a bodiless arm. I turned around to call Mami but I could not scream or move. I was frozen between the room and the skeleton and all the while Mami was calling me to return. I was standing right in front of her but she could not see me at all. She kept looking for me but she could not see me even though I was in front of her. It was as if I dematerialized in front of her. Suddenly, I was released, but not until grandmother Tita had left the apartment. I never found out why Tita came in the first place.

Mami never did mention to me why grandmother Tita came. All she could tell me was that it had something to do with mother.

Not all rooms were bad, of the four rooms; I did have one favorite room which I called the blue room. There was something peaceful about the blue room, which was further up from the middle room. This was my special room, the evil spirits would not enter, but that did not stop the cat size rats that found their way into my room.

There were three other bedrooms at Mami's house, and of those three, two were very significant; the middle room which I mentioned earlier and my favorite room. No one knows who painted the room blue but since Mami had so many visitors from church, some stayed longer than expected and during their stay, they decided to paint the room blue. This room was very special to me because if you placed yourself in the right space looking out the window, a person could see the top of the buildings but not just any building, you could see a church with a tall white cross on it. This, I truly enjoyed.

As a little girl, I would think I was on top of the world when I looked out the window. The blue room was my refuge and solace. I could see amazing things from its view. It was the second day of my stay with Mami that I had the privilege of enjoying a warm spring downpour, and like many of my past experiences, from years before; I knew that most likely I would get a glimpse of a rainbow. While the raindrops hit the windowpane and the lightning and thunder displayed their wonders, I began to think about whom I was, and why things happened to me.

I perched myself near the edge of the window, looking outside. It was my mission, at that very moment, to catch a glimpse of a rainbow. I believed in my heart that this was no ordinary rainbow. This rainbow would usually be seen in a special place. For some reason, rainbows would cast themselves over the upright cross of the church down the street. I think now it was because the building was white and the position of cross reflected light. However, regardless as to why this happened, it was a sight to behold. I thought it was fascinating to watch a rainbow right above a cross, as if it was meant to be there, and this day was no exception. After being gone for almost two years, the positioning of the rainbow did not change. What a comfort to know that the rainbow was the only thing that did not change and was steadfast. The rainbow knew where it belonged just like I did, next to Mami.

Thinking about the rainbow, and its significance, brought me consolation that there is still a God. My mind would drift into the

Bible stories told to me regarding the days of Noah [1] and the flood and why the world was destroyed. As a child, I heard many variations as to why, but one stuck in my head—*"wicked."* The people were wicked and had to be destroyed because they did bad things to each other, and God wanted to destroy them.

Processing all this information, I began to think, as to why God wouldn't destroy the people that hurt me now? However, for the moment, it was nice to be at Mami's home again, and being with her made me extremely happy. I belonged with Mami. Well, the day turned into one week. Toward the end of my stay, Mami called me into the room to ask me several questions. First, she started with a speech about liars and how Jesus does not like liars. Then she proceeded to tell me about my aunt Rita and how much Rita loves her children. She then asked me if I loved my cousins. *"How did you feel when your dad was not around?"* I answered her, saying that I understood about liars and that I felt bad that my dad was not around. Next she told me that she had heard a story about Edward doing some things to me, but to remember that if this story is true, my cousins may not have a father and to think about my cousins.

You see, the way that my story resurfaced was that Nelda sat both Lily and myself down and asked a series of questions. One of the questions that Nelda asked me was if anyone ever touched me the wrong way and so, I told her the truth. I told Nelda that Edward not only touched me he also did very painful things to me. I never did tell Nelda of what Marty *",the candy man,"* or Jane did to me because what Edward did to me could not be compared with the little damage Jane and Marty did to me so; I never mentioned them at all. Nelda told everyone in my family and now Mami was confronting me by asking some questions.

"Do you want your cousins to be raised without a father?" she asked?

"No!" I declared.

"Well, if it is true, that is what will happen. Did your Uncle Edward touch you?" After thinking, I replied that he had not. "You see, you were lying and Jesus does not like liars." At that very moment, I had mixed feelings about Mami. I felt betrayed by the only woman that I thought really loved me. Why would she want me to lie? My life changed after the talk with Mami.

Unwillingly, I was everyone's mental, emotional, and physical slave. It left me questioning myself, *"If God knows these things why would He allow it to continue? What did I do wrong? Why me? I guess I deserve to be touched and in pain because I must be a bad girl."* I think what bothered me most was that as a child, I was taught not to question the Lord, but I hated the way I felt because I did question God. I would try not to hate these individuals by being a good little Christian girl, allowing them to do whatever they wanted because I wanted to go to heaven. Is this the long-suffering that I must endure to make it in to heaven? *"Oh God will you come soon and take me away from these people?"* I would ask. I had no place to turn to. Mother was mentally disabled, my father had his own family now, and I could not find a way out. I would ask God to send me elsewhere and I would then again begin to think, *"Where else."* I could not go to Rita's house because she was married to Edward, my molester, and now, I was a liar. I mean, who would want a liar in their home especially one who lied about something as big as molestation? The thought that I went to Mami— the woman that I had loved all my life and she betrayed me, was heartbreaking to me. So, I gave up hope because I did not have a choice.

However, after *"the talk"* with Mami, every time someone did something to me, I became angrier towards my family, each and every one of them. There were so many emotions that I could not control, I wanted all my family members dead. I wanted my dog dead, my church dead, mother dead and anything that I had any feelings for, dead, and yet, another emotion that I felt was remorse. I knew that God did not want us to hate each other. But why would God allow this to happen to me in the first place?

What happened to the verse that said, do not harm children? *"And whoever receives one little child like this in My name receives Me. But whoever causes one of these little ones who believe in Me to sin, it would be better for him if a millstone were hung around his neck, and he were drowned in the depth of the sea"* (Matthew 18:5-6) NKJV. Did they forget to read this verse? It was my conversation with Mami that I developed a loathing towards God because this God of the children was double-minded and He was not merciful at all. How can a God Who loves His children allow this to happen to them? I was so angry with God.

Have you ever felt that way? Has anyone robbed you of your childhood, your innocence, and your faith in people?

After Mami's betrayal, life got even worse for me. A self-hatred began to manifest in me and I began to cut my arms to deal with my inner pain. The inner turmoil was by far more painful than that of the physical. I had no control at all. I could not bear to look in the mirror. Also, *"the candy man"* resumed molesting me again after so many years away from him. He started where he dropped off but this time the sexual abuse was conducted in my favorite blue room. Sadly, I never attempted to catch another glimpse of a rainbow from my blue room again. The very day that Marty began to molest me again was the day the rainbows ceased for me.

Chapter 5

Will It Ever End?

"The manner in which one endures what must be endured is more important than the thing that must be endured."

—DEAN GOODERHAM ACHESON

Where was my protector? Will it ever end? You've probably asked that question once or twice in your lifetime. For me, it was a constant question.

Dad was so busy with his own life, and new family, that he neglected me and I couldn't understand it. Nelda controlled everything in the house and in my life. Once again, dad was being controlled by another woman. Controlling my father was done by making sure that I was kept near Nelda at all times. I couldn't do anything without first going through Nelda. Nelda had so much control that if anyone was to give me anything they would have to give her daughter, Lily, something too. It did not matter that Lily could receive gifts from her own family and they could neglect me. One of Lilly's aunts even told me that the reason she could give Lily a gift and not me was because Lily is her niece and I wasn't. I thought, how cruel could she be? In fact, the whole family was cruel. This incident was small in comparison to the larger emotional abuses that I endured with Nelda's family, but it did not stop from hurting me nonetheless.

In addition, through this season of more pain, I ended up with three more molesters all before turning ten years old. The first was Mami's brother-in-law, Tony; he was in his late fifties. Second was Gustavo, in his forties, he too was another church deacon, and third, a nineteen year old boy from church.

Tony loved to fondle and kiss. This was very disgusting to me. The nineteen year-old young man, also liked to fondle and kiss. But Gustavo was not only a molester; he was a sexual predator. Dad took pity on Gustavo because his wife threw him out of the house and had nowhere to stay. So, dad asked him to stay at our home for a short-time. I knew there was something wrong, something was not right with him. Gustavo did not find interest in Lily but he gravitated to me. I didn't understand why, Lily was much cuter than me. I guess that he did not bother her because she did not play around and she spoke her mind in a minute. Maybe, that is why he thought that I might be an easier target, because I was usually the quiet one.

I tried to avoid him because I did not like him, something about him was terribly wrong. I found out how sick Gustavo really was when he showed me his collection of odd pictures. He would collect pictures from a local Spanish magazine of news and events. I do not know why, but this specific magazine showed pictures of little girls found dead, they were raped. He had a fascination of just staring at these little naked bodies lying in a pool of blood. He would show me these pictures for what reason, I cannot explain.

It did not take long before he attempted to rape me and then I understood why he would show me these pictures; he desired to do the same to me. But, he was really mistaken, I was much older and this time I spoke up. I have had enough! When dad found out that Gustavo not only tried to rape me but also attempted to dishonor Nelda, he threw him out of our house. I am not sure if dad did this because of me or because his wife was attacked, but at least it did show that dad was capable of protecting me for the second time in my life.

Odd thing however, I never had the courage to tell dad that Marty was still molesting me. I guess because I knew that Marty was paying my tuition, at a private school, and I felt indebted to him. Besides, the molestation did stop in the spring of my twelfth birthday because we were moving away. I was grateful to see the last of him!

Chapter 6

Massachusetts Here We Come!

"Our lives begin to end the day we become silent about things that matter." —MARTIN LUTHER KING

It was the summer of 1978 when Nelda decided that we should all move to Lancaster, Massachusetts, because she wanted to attend a Christian college. Lastly, after much planning, we moved to Lancaster Massachusetts in the early part of autumn, but without dad, he was to arrive later on that year. Immediately, I was given many responsibilities, and being the oldest, much was expected of me, including taking care of my new baby sister, Daniela. I must admit, the move did not help Lily, she became more unmanageable, but I bore the brunt of her actions. I tried to explain to Nelda that Lily was out of control. She was caught stealing and trying to forge a social security check at age ten. When I approached Nelda about this, Nelda began to hit herself on the face and on the head, in the middle of campus, while we were going to wash clothes. I was so embarrassed and felt sad for her. Her son Sammy was heading in the same direction and I was to watch over these little demons.

Dad finally made it to Massachusetts right before starting school and I was glad that he did. That year, academically, I was barely hanging on by a thread. Also, my attitude had shifted and it was not for the better. I was tired! I wanted to die! As if life could not get any worse, in the spring of 1979, Rita decided to leave Puerto Rico and move to Massachusetts as well, to attend the same college as Nelda.

Because of my change in attitude and lack of will, the family began rumors that I was a child with great mental issues because I had denied ever being molested to Mami. They thought that a child who could lie about such a thing must be sick. I began to have nervous breakdowns. I was turning thirteen years old that summer. Dad decided to take me to a psychologist to find out what was going on with me, however, dad did not drive so he would ask Edward, the rapist to take us. I would be mortified when Edward would take me by himself. He would take a detour around the cemetery and make statements like, *"It would be a shame for a girl your age to end up here."*

Arriving at the psychologist's office, I was sealed like a tomb. I would not say a thing. Therapy was useless because *"the rapist"* was sitting on the other side of the door. Internally, I was confused and dejected. My emotional and spiritual life began to end the moment I remained silent and nothing seemed to revive me.

Since I did not speak up to the psychologist, the family decided to take matters into their own hands and diagnose me. They concluded that I was a child with mental problems and a habitual liar. This made my life more unbearable. These were the very people that molded me and now are attempting to diagnose me. How incredible is that? Ignorance combined with education can be very dangerous and this is the case with Rita, because she studied psychology and attained her teaching credential, she was now an authority as to why I acted the way I did. Oh, I hated Rita with a passion. Just to think that I once loved her and now, I could not stand her. Sometimes Rita would make statements to me that she knew me more that I knew myself and I hated her for it. If she really knew me, she would have noticed how I acted toward

Edward. Also, if she paid close attention she would have seen how much I loved my cousins and the sacrifices that I made so that my cousins could have a good life.

Nelda's graduation day was creeping up very soon and she was already making plans to move again. In the spring of 1980, Nelda decided that she would like to continue her studies in San Diego, California. When I had heard about the move, I begged dad to keep me with him while Nelda settled in San Diego with her kids and her family. Dolores and Jose had moved out to San Diego several years earlier and now they wanted Nelda close to them. However, to make sure that my father would follow her to San Diego, Nelda insisted that I remain with her for security.

Chapter 7

California Here We Come!

"The real problem is not why some pious, humble, believing people suffer, but why some do not." —C.S. LEWIS

Dad agreed to Nelda's demands and we were off to San Diego. We arrived early summer and I was about to turn fourteen years old within a couple of weeks. We were picked up by Melvin a step uncle. Melvin was the youngest of Nelda's brothers. He was twenty-two years old, and he reminded me of a gigolo when he came to pick us up at the airport. He had a car that looked like it belonged to a pimp. San Diego, California was absolutely beautiful and again, I thought that maybe this would be a great change for all of us, but that was not the case. Jose hated me, but then again, he hated everyone in the name of Jesus Christ. Living in his house was torture. The unfortunate part was that everyone had me pegged as the bad kid who lied about everything.

Summertime came and it was enjoyable when leaving the presence of Jose. It was our first summer in San Diego and it was absolute paradise! We were exposed to the outdoors—pools, barbeques, and guys. Remember, I was turning fourteen years old, so boys became a focus for Lily and me. I noticed one day that my Uncle Melvin was looking at me differently, but I paid no attention because he was my step uncle. Summer ended faster than we liked. School started and Lily and I were extremely shocked. I never met a Mexican before and it was a rarity to see so many white kids in one location. Growing up in the Bronx, we were exposed to Blacks, Puerto Ricans and Dominicans and on occasion you may spot a white kid. It was hard being the only Puerto Rican at the school.

It seemed like a daily ritual that I had to defend Lily or myself. There was a lot of racial tension. The Mexican girls thought we were black, the black girls thought we were Mexican, and the *"white Girls, aka Valley Girls,"* did not care because they were in their own world. It was an insurmountable level of stress for anyone that had gone through what I went through, and now I was fighting to keep my sanity in school. I tried to be a Chola which is a Mexican gang member, but there was a problem, I am AmerRican. My parents were born in Puerto Rico with ancestors from Africa and Spain, hence, my extremely curly hair, full lips, natural assets and light-skin. I tried being one of the black girls but I was too white for them. I even attempted to be a *"Valley Girl,"* but I wasn't white, so it just didn't work out. I am AmerRican and I had to embrace who I was.

Fortunately and unfortunately, I had step aunts that were a couple of years older than me, so they came in and helped me with many fights. After a couple of months things began to settle at school. One thing bad about having young aunts was that they, too, were growing up and were experimenting with drugs and introduced me to marijuana.

I did experiment, and inhaled, but I felt that I could not let something else control my life. Unfortunately, that was not the case with Lily. She was hooked. In addition to my constant attempts, of trying to figure out who I was, I had to fight to keep Lily from smoking pot and getting into trouble. She was a handful. One day, she was in the restroom and I had to pull her out and physically hurt her because she got into trouble regardless of the situation, I would get in trouble and I was not going to have more problems than I already had. These young aunts were corrupting Lily. I soon realized that having young aunts could be a good thing, but I must say they were not the best example. We wanted to be like the younger of the two aunts and so we picked up habits that did not benefit us in the future. The youngest Aunt, Annie, was a tough cookie and she could care less who you were. If she needed to talk back to you, or anyone, she would. Lily became exactly like her in many ways.

Lily got very good at pushing my buttons and we would have real physical combat. After all, I would get into trouble when she did something so it was in my best interest, to keep her in line. In addition to Lily's awful behavior, I had to deal with Nelda. She and I would have many fights and arguments because of Lily's disrespect toward me and getting away with things. Things escalated when Nelda attempted to hit me one day. I physically fought back, and of course, it was them against me. Nelda kept telling me how awful of a child I was and that I'd better shape up. Fighting back did not benefit me at all. Nelda told all of her family that I had hit her back and they were upset with me which compounded their dislike for me except for Uncle Melvin—he listened to me and wanted the best for me.

I was tired of other people's physical, mental, and emotional baggage. I simply wanted to be a normal teenager.

Fall came and left and dad had not yet made it out to California. I grew closer and closer to Uncle Melvin because he treated us nieces like adults. Dad finally arrived in the winter and I was so relieved. It was Christmas of 1980, and things started to look as though they were going to turn around, but I had so much pressure still. During the traditional family Christmas party, Jose, *"the evil one,"* verbally and emotionally abused me in front of the whole family. I was in tears. I ran to the back of the apartments and broke down.

Melvin came following and tried to comfort me, but then he started kissing me on my lips. I pushed him away. He was not attractive at all and was kind of a mousy man, but, he seemed to have a good heart. He told me that he really liked me. It felt nice to hear this, but then I felt bad; the emotions came up again as before when something was not right. He said, *"It will be our little secret."* Again, I had to have another secret, but I thought to myself, *"could this be my knight in shining armor, coming to rescue me from all this? How could he like me, he has so many girlfriends?"*

He grabbed me by the hands and opened the garage unit. We continued to kiss and talk. I felt special for the first time in a long time, and he did comfort me, but I still had to tell Nelda because I was so confused.

Several weeks later—now—January 1981, I took the opportunity to speak with Nelda, like daughter to mother. What a big mistake. I told her that Melvin kissed me and she asked, *"Why would he do that."* I told her that I thought he liked me. She said she did not believe it. Once again, someone else was in a state of denial and I was being denied the right to speak my peace. Nelda asked me *"Why would my brother even think about being with you when he has so many beautiful girlfriends, did you come on to him?"* I explained that I was crying about things that were happening, at the Christmas party, and he came after me to console me and one thing led to the other. He was the first one to initiate the kiss, I did not. She said she would talk to him.

Apparently, they spoke because he approached me and told me, by the side of the house through my bedroom window, that he would like to see me but that I must keep it a secret., and , I said, *"okay."* We had a semi-sexual relationship, but never intercourse. I wanted to save myself for my marriage. Silly me! Melvin kept pressing on for about five months to go further and I would refuse. Then overnight, he began to treat me like a niece again. I was distraught. I decided to go to one of my younger aunts, Abbey, and

I explained to her what had taken place. She confronted him and he denied the whole thing in front of me. The words that came out of this man, about me and to me, were unbelievable. *"Everyone knows that she is a liar and this is just another one of her lies. She is sick in the head and I would never do something like that with something like her."* Some—Thing? That is what I was...a thing? *"How could you believe her over me?"* he asked. He called me all kinds of names and treated me like garbage. Melvin was an Amnon in my life.

A couple of months passed and I had just turned fifteen years old. I found out that during the time Melvin was trying to have sex with me, he was grooming Lily. Then I learned the truth about Melvin. He was a sexual predator. I am so glad that I never really went all the way with Melvin. It was during this time, as well, that I realized what had happened. I did not love him, but I loved the fact that he treated me so nice at the beginning. I thought I needed that kind of affection. All that changed when he began to date his own blood cousin, Vicky, who was seventeen years older at the time. Nelda was so happy for them. The three of them turned my world upside down. In dad's house, they would call me names and Nelda would allow it. To my surprise, Melvin proposed to Vicky that same year.

Hell was at home. Anything outside of home was heaven. I took on a summer job to get out of the house and make money for myself. I loved to buy nice business clothes and look good because my parents never had any money. But it did not stop Nelda from buying nice things for her precious Lily. Needless to say, Lily got into more trouble and pushed my buttons more and more each day. From my perspective, Lily had everyone's blessings to do what she wanted. Melvin even told her that if I were ever to lay my hands on her, that he would take care of me. So, this was carte blanche for Lily. It was difficult for me because on one hand, I had Lily and her attitude and Nelda on the other hand controlling every step I made. I told dad about what was going on but he just wouldn't listen to me.

One day dad was not able to take the pressure of our constant discourse. It seemed like each day Nelda found ways to cause an argument about me. I guess dad had enough of Nelda because while I was sitting in the living room watching television he told me to turn off the television. I did not understand why I had to turn the television off if I had done everything that Nelda requested of me. It never failed, this always happened when Lily did not complete her chores and then everyone would suffer. So dad demanded that I turn the television off and I did not, it was not right. Nelda continued instigating, in the background, and when dad came over to me, he grabbed me by the neck, and began to choke me, telling me that I had to listen to him. I was in shock that my own dad, knowing that I was a good kid, would do this for Nelda. The woman did not even love him. That was it... I was not going to let my own father abuse me too.

I called the police, and I ended up in Juvenile Hall. That was the beginning of police officers coming to our home. As I went to the hall, I thought about how I got there. I also thought about the kind of people that I had in my life...they really were sick. Why? Where was God?

Several days passed; when I was picked up by my father. Nothing of course changed, but he never did that again. Now that I had gone to juvenile hall, Lily could not hold that information to herself. This is the same girl that at ten years old tried to cash our neighbor's social security check and never got in trouble for it. Lily was bad to the bone. She told everyone that I had gone to juvenile hall, and what was left of my reputation was destroyed. The church members knew, so did the staff in school, the neighbors, and anyone that had ears. Either Nelda or Lily told them and for a whole year I could not live this incident down. Everything I did was wrong, so I delved into school and the following summer I worked to get out of the house. That same year, I was awarded a scholarship to a business school but Nelda was not at all happy, because Lily was not doing well in school. When I was offered the scholarship I was ecstatic. It was a business program that I had entered and I was doing excellent, but dad declined. Yet, Lily was attempting to get into modeling school during the same time and Nelda was excited! She considered sending Lily but couldn't afford the tuition. I was depressed, so I worked and focused on the first day of school and getting involved in extracurricular activities. I was trying to live a peaceful life but it was impossible. I was living in a house filled with insane family members, and they were in control. Summer was over and I looked forward to getting back to school and to my friends. I knew that I could find some peace, at least, in school.

One day, Lily was not having a good day, and when she did not have a good day, everyone in the house suffered. I did all my work at home, as required of me, and Lily would not do her part. If she did not do her part then all of us kids would be punished. For one reason or another, Lily pushed a button that set me off. I hit her, and the reason that I did, was because she said, *"You can't do anything to me because if you do, my uncle Melvin will take care of you."* With that, I said, *"Yeah,"* and began to pound her. It's not like we weren't the same height, and weight. We were only two years apart, so it was not like I was hitting a younger, defenseless person.

After our physical combat, everything calmed down. About two days passed when Melvin and Vicky came to visit, which was odd, but I paid no mind. Nelda was comforted by Vicky. Melvin wanted to speak with me in private. As we entered the room, he began to insult me and I told him that I did not have to take it. I began to walk out when Melvin grabbed me and began to punch me with a closed fist all over my body. He kicked me, threw me against the wall, and slapped me on my face, in my father's house.

I was screaming for my stepmother to come and rescue me, but no one ever came. It seemed like forever; then he finished and walked away. The only thing that was said to me by Nelda was, *"You don't put your hands on my daughter, and if you do it again, this will happen again."* I was in shock! Lily was Nelda's pride and joy and no one was to touch her precious Lily.

When my father came home and found out, he did something that I could not believe. What did my father do? I would like to say that he took a stand but that did not happen. The next thing I remember was being sent to Rita's house, who now lived in Michigan. Here I went again; being pawned off on someone else. To summarize my feeling at that time- I felt like a piece of human luggage, carrying my internal issues along with the emotional baggage others had placed on me.

Chapter 8

Forgiven By My Molester!

"One should rather die than be betrayed. There is no deceit in death. It delivers precisely what it has promised. Betrayal, though ... betrayal is the willful slaughter of hope." —STEVEN DEITZ

It was now late summer of 1982, and yes, I was going back to my aunt Rita's house who now lived in Michigan, while she was attending another Christian University. I did not know what to expect. This is the very aunt whose husband raped me when I was eight years old. However, I thought that anything was better than living with Lily and Nelda. Upon my arrival, my Aunt Rita was cordial with me. We had idle conversations, but nothing real. Rita asked what had happened to me and I simply told her the truth—but because of a troubled past and the lie that Mami forced me to live with; she did not really believe me. She had to see the evidence and not until she saw the bruises on my body did she believe me. Rita then called Mami and confirmed what she had seen. They were both very angry at what had happened to me.

As always, I tried to find the positive side in almost every situation so, at least, I was excited to see my cousins Catherine, Edward Jr., Danny and the youngest of the cousins Patrick and re-acquaint myself with them. My love for my cousins was extremely profound and I would do anything for them. I felt that by sacrificing me, at least they would be safe. My cousins were safe with both their parents and no one would ever hurt them like I had been hurt. I took pride in the fact that I had a large part in keeping them safe, therefore I continued to keep quiet.

Seeing my cousins after so many years did make me feel that I had done something good for them. Now that I was sixteen years old I thought that nothing could happen to me and all was behind me, but I was still unsure of what would happen to me if the truth ever came out. A week passed by when the inevitable happened—Rita asked me, for the first time, about the *"incident."* *"Did my husband do anything to you when you were a little girl because everyone heard about it?"*

I remembered the conversation with Mami regarding my cousins being fatherless and I feared that I would be thrown out into the streets if I were to say yes. Why? Because there were so many uncertainties, so I said NO, once again. She looked at me with anger and said, *"Do you know what you have done to my husband's reputation? You lied! You will need to ask him for forgiveness. I am ashamed. You even told our neighbor's kid, who told me what you said about my husband, 'How embarrassing."* My life was so full of uncertainties I would rather continue denying it because I did not know what would happen to me next. All I could say to Rita was, *"I am sorry,"* even though I knew that Edward did rape me.

When Edward arrived from work that evening, Rita greeted him and told him that he needed to speak with me. He asked about what? Rita told him it was about *"the incident"* when I was a little girl. Edward, looking scared said, *"I thought we determined that it was a lie."* Rita said that she had to know and asked me now that I am much older. He asked me to step into the bedroom with him, and in a split second, I felt like that little girl again being escorted into the room by Edward the rapist.

I sat on one side of the bed and he sat on the other. He asked me, *"So, what do you want to talk to me about?"* Inside, I was praying and hoping that Edward would confess that he did rape me. Edward looked at me and I looked down and said, *"I am sorry for lying about you, please forgive me."* These were, in fact, the hardest words that I had ever had to regretfully say. Inside, I was praying again that Edward would say, *'No, I need to be forgiven by you because I did rape you,'* but that did not happened. Edward smiled and said, *"I FORGIVE YOU."* In my mind, I was saying, *"What? You jerk, you raped me, and I know it. I felt it."* Internally, I was questioning him, *"How could you sit there?"* but externally I put myself aside and said thank you. Edward had betrayed me and I could not forgive him. What happened next blew my mind. Edward actually asked that we kneel down and pray. Once again, my mind was saying, *"What?"*

He opened up the prayer with *"Dear heavenly Father, we come to you because there has been a lie committed, and I pray that you would forgive "Grace."* I want her to know that I forgive her and that I love her. All these things we pray, in Jesus name, amen. Edward betrayed me and that day, my hopes and dreams were slaughtered.

I hated both God and Jesus at that very moment. In my eyes, they were not fit for my loyalty or my worship. I had developed such a hate so great, but no one would have ever guessed, because I went through the motions of going to church and all. What was left of my credibility, in the family, no longer existed and now it was confirmed that I was truly a liar. Did they not see that I only wanted to be loved? I wished that at the time someone would have said, 'I love you because of who you are not who I want you to be.'

After several months with Rita, I was shipped off to my older aunt, Lisa who lived in New York. It was January 1983. Lisa was a God fearing woman who hated life and everyone in the world. To me, she was just another version of Jose and mother. Living with Lisa taught me to hate myself; whatever was left, of me, to love, was totally diminished. My belief system was destroyed. Will this ever end? How could God allow this to happen to me again and again? What is wrong with God? But still I pressed on even though thoughts of suicide began to plague me day and night. Sometimes I would be by the train tracks and think that I should end my life. Other times, I began to entertain the idea of becoming a prostitute. Here I could make money and live in peace because the streets seemed to be much nicer than my family. At least, a prostitute is a prostitute and there is no lying about it, but one professing to be a Christian, physically hurting someone and lying about it was worse in my opinion.

    I hated life and each day that I would wake up; I wondered why I am still here? What have I done to deserve to be in this family and be forgiven by my molester? I remained with Lisa for several months, during which time I had a great idea- why not visit my biological mother and sisters? My aunt took me to a church where mother was a member. Mother greeted me very cordially and so did my sister Rachel. By this time she was twelve years old. Mother invited me to eat at her house and also spend the night. Rachel and I talked and laughed about everything and mother sat looking at us smiling. I seriously thought that mother would have changed by now and if so, I could finally be with her again but, my visit ended abruptly when mother's demons, once again, showed themselves. The second time I went to visit mother again, she told me to never come back again. Mother said, *"I hate you and as of today, I have only one daughter, and you are dead to me."* The reason I was dead to her was because she tried to tell me that she never abused me and I told her on the contrary and she could not handle the truth.

    The only hope I had of not losing my mind was to start visiting one of Nelda's younger sisters, Annie. She had gotten married and relocated to the Bronx from San Diego. Annie's house is where

I got to know another step uncle, Walter, who would visit when he had the chance. Walter was the eldest of the eight biological siblings and I respected him. Walter and I would speak about what happened between his younger brother Melvin and me, and how it was all a mistake. I told him how I wanted to move on and forget about the whole thing and go back home at any cost.

California—that is all I could think about at the time, but Nelda did not want me to return because I was too much trouble. Wait a minute! It was Melvin who beat me and tried to do bad things to me; yet I could not return to my dad's house? I wanted to know how to get back to California. Strategy was the key. I wrote a letter to Nelda, apologizing to her, and apologizing to Lily. Was this insane? Yes, but I had to go back. I wasn't going to school, and it was not because of my choosing. Unfortunately, Rita sent my transcripts to Lisa's home, along with all my documentation, to enter into school and they mysteriously disappeared, in fact, they never got to my aunts house. In the meantime all I would do is sit at Lisa's house all day. Day after day doing nothing and I was bored to death.

Although, I am a native New Yorker, I was accustomed to sunny California. I could not stand the winters, the isolation from everyone and I could not take another day with Lisa and her holier than thou attitude. Deep inside, she wanted to commit suicide and hated everyone around her.

Nelda received the letter, and accepted my apologies. Before I left to California, I even picked up gift favors for the soon to be newlyweds, Melvin and Vicky, for the wedding because they requested it. I did not care that I had to apologize to them and bring them their items. I was on my way back to California! On May 8, 1983, in time for Mother's Day, I went back home. How ironic!!!

Time of Self-Actualization

Chapter 9

The Psych Ward: My Happy Home

"Insanity is often the logic of an accurate mind overtaxed."
—OLIVER WENDELL HOMES

I wish that I could say that while I was away from my father that things changed at home but that was not the case. I knew that I did not come back to a loving family. It was a place to rest my head and wait for the day that I could leave. Lily got a little closer to me; however, it was all a charade. Lily was still running the house and more so than ever before. I hooked up with old friends from school and attempted to get back into the groove of things; without much success. Subsequently, at the home of my friend, who lived not too far from me, I met a young man in his early twenties from Trinidad, I had just turned seventeen and we fell in love. Or should I say, I fell in love? We continued to date for about ten months. He is the one that I gave my all; but after I gave my mind, body and soul, he left me for another girl.

I was devastated and I tried to talk with Nelda, telling her I had fallen from grace and that I was brokenhearted. Her response should not have surprised me but it did. Nelda told me that now I was a woman, and that I must start to act like one. *"When you get down with a man,"* as she used to put it, they do not need you anymore. After that day, she would remind me that I was no longer a virgin, and that was the straw that broke the camel's back. I attempted suicide with pills; instead I ended up with a bad hangover. I called Saundra, Lily's boyfriend's mother. She picked me up from my parent's home and nursed me all night long. Saundra was a good soul, even though her children were as messed up as I was, at the time. I guess that is why she took me under her wing. She called my parents that night to tell them that I was okay, but that I was feeling pretty sick. If it wasn't for Saundra and her help that evening, I may have attempted suicide again.

About two days later, I went back home and spoke to our neighbor who happened to be a nurse. She called the paramedics and they checked me and I was okay. That very week, a cop stopped by my house to speak with me. I did not know who he was but he heard about my failed suicide and made an effort to console me but his tactics were all wrong. He told me I would never amount to anything at the rate that I was going. That he has seen plenty of girls like me messing their lives up and I was heading the same direction. Meanwhile, I was thinking if you only knew buddy. If you only knew what hell I am in, you would take me out of this house and place me in a foster home. I was determined to show him, others and most importantly, myself, that I am not like the girls he mentioned or the sick girl that my family thought of me. I had to merely survive until I turned eighteen years of age.

Nelda took my attempted suicide as an opportunity to seal her ill feelings for me and made plans. Dad, Nelda, and I were scheduled to meet a psychologist at a hospital in Hillcrest, California. We went inside, I was asked a couple of questions, and then the psychologist said, *"You will remain with us until we know that you are okay."* I told Nelda, dad and the doctor, that I was okay, but the doctor sent for an orderly to watch me go to the restroom. I was trying to escape and I realized that they were not going to fall for it. I was being admitted into a psychiatric unit. Great!

The first day was scary for me; I had to change into clothes that they gave me and was stripped away from all my belongings. I was now in the closed unit and I could not sleep. There were so many kids and they all had the same issues. They were hurting souls, like me. One of the girls kept saying that she was pregnant, but she was not. She was in a world that could not be reached. All she would say was, *"save my baby please,"* as she would hold her belly.

As always, I made my environment a little bit better by adjusting. I lasted one day in the closed unit and then I was transferred to the open unit. Therapy went well and I liked it because of the structure. I befriended many kids in my unit, but some of the nurses were not so nice. During one of my therapy sessions, a nurse asked me about my childhood and I told her about one incident, the *"rape."* She said that maybe I was a promiscuous child and because of my promiscuity Edward raped me. What! Oh my Goodness, this woman does not know what she is talking about. How could an eight year old lure a man to molest her? That day, was when I stopped speaking with her about anything and spoke only to my therapist. I kept thinking, what the heck is going on with people?

I remember a young boy about my age, which would sit down and stare at his watch all day and night. I began to speak with him by asking him for the time. Days went by, and I sat with him and asked him questions; he would reply with a yeah or no and I thought great! Each day, for one month, he would open up little by little, and one day he laughed. I was so excited! In fact, I was asked by the staff to continue what I was doing. I did not continue because they asked me to, but because I thought he was quite interesting. There was a reason he closed up and I wanted to know why? What could be so bad that one would close up to the world? Well, unfortunately he never did tell me what his problem was, but we talked about many other things and one day, he hugged me and he left the unit.

The duration of my stay came to an end when my doctor thought I was ready to be released. I did not want to go! I imagine what kind of a nightmare my life was? The fact that I desired to remain in a psychiatric ward rather than go free should have alerted the doctors. Staying in a place that had structure and discipline was something I desired all my life. The ward was a place where all my basic needs were being met. But the unavoidable happened and I was being released. On the day of my release, from the open unit, dad and Nelda were already in the doctor's office when I walked in. The doctor assessed me and told my parents that I was a normal teenager and that they needed to remove the responsibilities of raising my siblings and being the second mom at home. *"Grace needs love and attention and she is the last one getting the attention. She is a normal seventeen year old with normal teenage issues."*

Suddenly there was an interruption by Nelda and she said to my father, *"I have to tell you something right now...our daughter is pregnant"* dad looked at me and I said, *"please, do not look at me."*

The doctor was in shock and so was dad because this time was to be used to talk about me and how things needed to change, but Nelda used this opportunity to tell dad that Lily was pregnant. I then told the doctor, *"You see doctor, Nelda, hated me so much that she tried to make me look like the bad kid, she focused on what I was doing, but neglected to discipline Lily, and now, Lily is pregnant at age fifteen."* Nelda did not listen to me when I would tell her what Lily was doing. The doctor looked at both my parents and told them that they needed to begin therapy, with Lily, as soon as possible. Nelda and dad looked at the doctor as if he was crazy to even suggest such a thing. I could not believe them, I looked at the doctor and asked him if I was released; he said yes. I turned around and told my parents, *"You guys suck as parents and I cannot wait to get out of the house, you guys are sick."* The doctor tried to persuade them to begin attending therapy sessions, but in their eyes, they did not have a problem. I walked out with my head up high for the first time in my life.

Chapter 10

The Era of Errors

"The only real mistake is the one from which we learn nothing." —JOHN POWELL

The year was quiet because of Lily's unplanned pregnancy. No one could say much, except Dolores, Lily's grandmother, who said to me, *"I thought you would have been the first to get knocked up."* What can I say, Delores was an insane woman. On the other hand, I was thrilled to find out that Uncle Walter had relocated to California, and hoped that he would become my advocate. He was the only one, from that whole family, who was nice to me. However, I should have realized by this time that no one in Nelda's family was ever nice to anyone unless they needed something. Sure enough, his intentions manifested in time.

I reached out to Uncle Walter for advice because he was much older than me. In fact, I had turned eighteen and he was twenty-nine years old. I knew I could count on him to guide me. But nothing prepared me for the relationship that began between us. Within months, I was pregnant with Walter's child; unfortunately, I miscarried. Times were turbulent for us because I soon realized that Walter was an alcoholic; but I was going to change him. The second pregnancy came, and this time, he threatened me if I did not abort the pregnancy, so I did.

Of course, Nelda was not at all happy with our relationship. Now, I was not only her step daughter but there was a great possibility that I would become her sister-in-law. Nelda would tell Walter stories about me—that I was spoiled and that I was a troublemaker. She made sure Walter understood that I was not a nice person and to be careful with me. In fact, she became *"the snitch"* because she would tell Walter that I would go and visit my girlfriend, who lived on the same block as I did. Nelda knew that her brother was a very jealous man, but she still did not care.

Not only was Walter jealous, he was abusive, and controlling. This did not matter to me because with my love, I thought I would change him. It was more like he was changing me rather than me changing him. Not only did I suffer a terrible childhood, now I embarked on a life of domestic violence, rape, forced abortions, and more emotional, verbal, and physical abuse. Meanwhile, amidst all of the abuse, I thought, at least I was out of my parent's home.

I was with Walter from the age of eighteen to twenty-eight years of age. Throughout our relationship, his alcoholism dictated how and where we would live. Walter had no respect for me, let alone my body. He would rape me even when I fought back. The word *"no"* was not respected, and I hated him for forcing himself on me and not thinking that his actions could impregnate me. And when he impregnated me, which was several times, his answer to my pregnancies was to get an abortion or don't come home. On June 11, 1985, my oldest daughter was born and I was a proud mother. Unfortunately, her birth did not change Walter's attitude and he continued to take advantage of me whenever he wanted.

After a second miscarriage and second abortion, I became pregnant, in February, 1987, with my youngest daughter. He did not want anything to do with my last pregnancy and neglected his responsibilities as a father. He was distant with me and would tell me that I robbed him of his youth. Here was a man that was eleven years older than me and I robbed him of his youth. Once again, I was reasoning with insanity and insanity was winning.

For a short-time, Walter's behavior toward me changed, when the baby came, but within a month or so, the arguments resumed and he decided to relocate to Sacramento, to be with his mother Dolores and his father Jose.

Unfortunately, Walter said that he would change and that things might be better for us in a new location so I packed up and moved to Sacramento, California, as well. In the spring of 1988, we got married, but, he was still irresponsible and did not care about anyone but himself.

Walter had a knack for quitting or getting fired from his jobs. His drinking became so unpredictable, that sometimes I would not see him for days. We experienced a cycle of violence which then led to a honeymoon period. My fear of Walter became more and more real. I would do anything he told me for fear of repercussions. He put me in very bad situations, like using Mami's credit card to cover expenses due to his lack of employment.

Walter was a natural when it came to threatening me, from minimal threats like not paying Mami's credit card debt, to paying me to sleep with him in order to obtain money to purchase groceries; not to mention, his violent threats. Walter would threaten me by showing actual footage of a woman called Maritza Martin Munoz [1] being shot to death by her former husband on national television. He would play it over and over again while warning me that he would do that to me if I left him. He even purchased a gun. I was scared for my life. He would threaten me with death, and constantly reminded me that if I attempted to leave him, our daughters lives would be in jeopardy; no matter how small the situation or incident.

Parenting my daughters was like raising someone else's children, because I really did not have any rights as a mother. All child rearing rights were Walter's. He would say to the girls, *"I do not care what your mother tells you, it is what I tell you that matters."* I felt like I was a concubine, not a mother.

The times that I would threaten to leave, he would tell me he would rather die and take the kids with him than to leave me with them. I did leave many times when I thought that I had had enough; nevertheless, he would find me or I would come back. No one dared to help me for they too, were in fear of any altercation with him. I must give credit to Vicky, Rose, Nelda and even Gladys for trying to help me escape numerous times, but no one took me seriously because I kept coming back.

His drinking became more and more constant, and there were nights that he would not call or come home, sometimes, I would not see him for days. I would find myself calling hospitals, family homes, and such. Sometimes I would find him, but most times, he was nowhere to be found.

It was during this time that I met a young man named Charles and I attempted to have an affair but it did not work. Charles was an honorable man and we broke it off before it became serious. After Charles, came Steven. Steven was the son of a sister from church. Steven was also in a relationship and had two sons of his own. At first, we began Bible studies together, but one thing led to another and we found ourselves consumed in lust not love.

Finally I found someone that would make me happy and might stand up to Walter. I tried to leave Walter again and I even broke it off with Steven because I wanted to keep my family. However, the more Walter would abuse me the more I desired Steven.

I did not want to leave Walter for the sake of the girls. I thought that if I would ever get the guts to really leave him that I might not be able to protect my daughters like Walter could. This thinking stemmed from my childhood; I was scared of everyone. What if someone raped my daughters; what if someone hurt them like I was hurt? The constant reminder of what he would do to me and what was done to me, as a child, drove me insane. My mind could not handle the abuse any longer, and then to make matters worse, I was getting pressured from Walter and the pastor.

Walter attempted to salvage our marriage by getting baptized in the same church that I belonged to. It is amazing what a spouse will do when they are losing ground. After trying and trying to get back together, I realized, there was no hope in mending this broken marriage. He was not willing to give up his drinking, and I was not willing to be abused any longer, and the fighting continued. At times I ended up staying at homeless shelters because of the abuse. During this time, Steven was worried for my life and told me that he wanted to marry me. Now, I was torn between two men and my past.

The baptism was Walter's last attempt to keep me, but, by this time Steven and I were in an extramarital affair. My intentions, at the time, were to never leave any doors open for Walter to come back. The evangelical pastor from my church had a talk with us to try to change my mind, but the truth came out as to why Walter really got baptized. Walter told the pastor that he got baptized to keep me and make me happy. The pastor was appalled at Walter's response, and let me say, that, I had some choice words with the pastor before I left his office. I could not believe that even with the reported abuse and his true confession, as to why he got baptized, the pastor wanted me to stay with Walter.

I just couldn't, I needed to find happiness for the first time in my life. I thought this was an opportunity for Steven and me to be together and build our life. I finally left my husband for Steven which was the worse decision I ever made. I should have left Walter and stayed by myself. After all was said and done, Steven did not have the same plans as I did. I was left alone to struggle with my daughters and I deserved it for being stupid, so I thought. Here I was without a husband and alone—not that I wanted Walter back—not at all. I would ask myself, if Steven loved me why would he want me practically out on the streets with my kids?

I was confused and hurt again. Here, I was fighting once again, but now I was fighting for my daughters and for myself.

Frantically, I was seeking shelter for all of us and the babysitter was kind enough to offer temporary shelter. She and her husband lived on the same property where my husband and I lived. Luck was short lived when my babysitter's husband, Ricardo, wanted more than I was willing to give (I was beginning to loath being a woman). I was in my room when Ricardo knocked and he asked to come in. I was apprehensive; something wasn't right and I thought what now?

Almost immediately I felt uncomfortable. *"I have been meaning to talk to you for some time, and I know this may be a sin but I desire you, I have tried to get these feelings out but, I think that you and I can be together."* Oh my, I am not the most beautiful woman in the world. I never gave him any indication that I desired him. I did not know what to think or even what to say. I was praying that he would not put his hands on me. I felt anguish that I could not do anything if he attempted to force himself on me. I felt distressed and I feared that this incident would compromise our shelter. I told him that I was in love with Steven and that we were hoping to be together. Ricardo asked me, *"If Steven loves you so much then why are you living here with us?"* He was not one of the smartest men I had ever met, but he did have a point. He tried to tell me that Steven did not love me, but that he could give me what I needed, without his wife knowing it. Again, secrets!

I politely asked Ricardo to leave my room and I prayed that this new incident would go away quickly. It was a mess. I would love to say that it was all in my imagination, but, unfortunately, it was not. I strongly believe that when a person is going through deep emotional problems, that they are indeed experiencing spiritual attacks. These *"attacks"* will make a person or break a person. At times the person may seem to walk around with an invisible sign that says *"please take advantage of me please, I am already down and can't get up at all."* I asked God, why this? Why now?

Thank goodness that there was a light at the end of the tunnel when my friend Jean Taylor, from my previous employment, allowed me to stay in her home until I could get situated. She was so awesome and I owe her my thanks and more. She opened her doors to my daughters and me with no strings attached. This act of kindness was the first of many blessings to come.

A couple of months went by and I went to Steven's job, and told him that I had done my part to show how much I loved him and that he must show me that he loved me by helping me move into an apartment. He helped me and I found an apartment in Citrus Heights, CA. and moved in with my daughters, away from Walter, and was enjoying freedom.

Like any stalker, Walter found out where I lived and began to cause me anxiety again. Life was a constant rollercoaster ride. The days of sleeping with Walter to get money for groceries or the bare necessities were over. Walter would not even give us money for food not even for his daughters. One day Walter came with $18.00 in his pocket for groceries. In fact, Walter had so much control over his own family that no one, from his family, wanted to help me, with the exception of his cousin Vicky. She was the only person, from my youth, who gave me $20.00. Another time one of his sisters, Rose, the one that did not like me because of her racial issues, found it in her heart to give me $20.00 and told me not to ever say anything to him.

I could not handle all that strife by being nice to Walter, because the nicer I was to him, the more he would manipulate the situation. Sometimes, we did not have anything to eat, and I would have to look through seat cushions, for change, to buy .99 cent tacos so the girls could eat. I called dad to see if they could take care of the girls until I picked myself up and he declined. I swore to my father that if I lost custody of my girls he would never see me again. All I desired was to get back on my feet. I was not using drugs, sleeping around and or nightclubbing. I merely needed a little help for the time being. Dad and Nelda declined. Every door was closing in on me.

It was a nightmare and I had to think how to resolve my problems all the while the bills started piling up. I was losing ground because I was limited in my education, no experience, no transportation and absolutely no funds.

After almost a year of struggling financially and being scared to file for child support, in 1995, I gave my daughters to Walter under joint custody, with the promise that he would give the girls back to me when I got on my feet. I knew that if Walter had the girls, he would not stalk me and he would not be harassed by the court to pay for child support, but most importantly, no one would ever dare hurt the girls. Also, he threatened my life if I even considered filing for child support.

As fate would have it, during this time, my apartment burned down while at a funeral in San Diego; Marvell's husband passed away. Since the girls were taken care of by Walter, I had nothing to hold me back so I decided to move to San Diego to be with Marvell and her two little girls. I was technically homeless, mainly living out of my car and staying at a friend's home. Homelessness was better than living with Walter but that never stopped me from missing my daughters with every fiber of my being. I knew that I was free from Walter's abuse and also that my daughters were safe with him. Walter had no reason to stalk me, abuse me, hurt me, or rape me anymore. But that did not stop Walter; since he could not control me any longer he used the court system and filed for child support. This meant that he got on welfare. The only reason that Walter was successful in obtaining full custody of my daughters was because he perjured himself by telling the family court that I abandoned my children. Walter did not want to go through the channels of communication that I had in place, to avoid stalking from Walter. His perjury was a direct retaliation towards me because he lost control of me.

Walter knew that in the event of an emergency, he was to call my dad, Nelda or Marvell but since he did not have control, he used the courts to do his dirty work. Because of this, I was sued for child support and faced parental alienation. Walter used everything in his arsenal to get back at me and he got away with murder. He played dirty and used others to help him. Walter was the epitome of a wife beater but made himself look like the victim.

I left everything behind in Sacramento to find a normal life. The constant memories from my childhood and all the abuse as an adult did not allow me to be happy for a very long time. I was going through a process of refining to learn from, or to die from. It was my *"era of errors"* and nothing was going to change unless I decided to make better decisions. It seemed that *"the decisions that I made in life whether good or bad had a way of controlling my life. I knew that I had to choose wisely to stop the madness."* My question to you today is, have you learned from your past mistakes? What decisions do you have to make that will change the course of your life for the better?

Chapter 11

A Chair Is Still a Chair

"Cemeteries are our final destinations. They are full of regrets, lost hopes, unfulfilled dreams, and missed opportunities. Don't wait to be in the presence of your abuser, molester or rapist to forgive them. Forgive them regardless if they are dead, alive, near or far, just forgive them before you reach… your final destination." —VIVIONNE "GRACE" KELI

How can I stop making the same mistakes time after time? I was sick of making mistakes and also, I was fed up with the time that I had lost on each and every one of them. I thought how come I keep attracting the wrong people into my life? I knew that I had a treasure within me and in order to find my treasure within, I had to accept and move on from the past. Life as I knew it began to crumble before my eyes and finding my treasure within felt unattainable.

More things happened to me once I left Walter and relocated to San Diego, California. From the latter part of 1995, I began to take an expansive look at my life to try and figure out how much of my life was dictated by others, in my past, and how much is my doing. I knew that I could not continue to use my past as a crutch and that I had to be accountable for my life sooner or later. I did not want to be like Walter or others in my past that blamed everyone else. It was important to be responsible and a vital member of society— not a burden.

Things started to change once I began taking responsibility for my own actions. Time went by and in the beginning of 1996, things began to look manageable. I was ready to be sociable again. I had kept in contact with old friends from Sacramento. One particular person was Craig, a young man that I had met while working at the Department of Human Services in Sacramento, several years earlier. Craig was an intake worker for a non-profit organization next door to where I was working at the time. Our friendship was strictly platonic. While living with Marvell in San Diego, Craig called me one day to tell me that he had relocated to Los Angeles and wanted to see me and catch up. He was living with his grandmother and was working at a women's shelter, in downtown Los Angeles, as a psychologist. He asked me out and I thought why not. We went on several trips together on the weekends. On one of our trips we were passing through the desert, on our way back from Arizona, the long stretch of highway was really isolated with few cars seen. It was around dusk, Craig stopped his jeep and looked at me, I asked him what was on his mind but he did not say anything. It appeared to me that he was going to ask me something or get out of the car and stretch but the look in his eyes did not make any sense to me. I brushed it off.

Several months after our trip to Arizona, I moved into a home, where I rented a room from a young lady near La Jolla, California. One day, Craig called me and asked me if he could come over my new place and I said yes. The odd thing however, is that Craig emphatically requested that I tell no one he would be visiting me that weekend. He actually made me promise him that I wouldn't. I found that to be an unusual request so I told Marvell because something told me that something was not right.

In fact, it was a weekend when my roommate would be out of town skiing so, the house would be all for me and my guest. Nevertheless, I thought we could actually have clean fun. Craig arrived late which was unusual for a punctual person like him. It was not a good sign, when he came over with hard liquor knowing that I did not drink. I could not understand why he would do this. He was nervous and unsettled not his usual, loving self. Craig also made mention of how long he had liked me, but because I was going through so much with Steven and my former husband he had chosen to leave me alone.

Craig also spoke to me about how he hated the way I would talk to my daughters when he and I spoke in the past, during our phone conversations. I was thinking that this was several years ago why this conversation now? I told him that I was not in the best of mental health when he first met me. Our conversations began like a psychological session gone wrong. I had to reassure him that my life was getting much better and I had plans to really do great things. He kept dwelling on Steven, and the fact that I did not have my daughters with me. Then he switched, as if to say that he had enough of my responses. He then asked me who knew he was visiting me. I lied and said no one knew that he was coming over. He then began to coerce me to drink; all the while I was thinking this is odd. Silly me, I obliged because I thought that maybe he was having a hard day. I went along with it but then he continued to pour more and more and started to ask me questions about Steven again and how he really liked me, but that it could never be. It was then that he reached for his shaving kit bag and pulled out what appeared to be silver duct tape, a set of gloves and a short piece of rope. Oh my, this is not what I was hoping for at all. How can this man be like this and he works with homeless women in a shelter?

Craig started becoming rough with me and pushing me around so, I told him, that I lied, I did tell my best friend, but he would not listen and he began to wrestle me to the bed. He was trying to tie me up, and the more I fought the more aroused he would get. I stopped and used reverse psychology, by making him believe that I was being aroused as well. I grabbed his groin and sure enough he was turned off and was angry that I did that. He gathered his materials and I never saw him again. All I know is that he was not himself that night and I really do not know what he would have done to me that night. It was hard to believe that this man was working in a well-known and reputable women's shelter, in Downtown Los Angeles. The very fact that he had access to records and women was disturbing to me.

This situation left me thinking...What did Craig, see in me, that he thought he could try to take advantage of me, and God knows what else; since he was so adamant that no one know that he was in my home. Well, life went on and I had to brush myself off and continue my quest. Not too long after the attempted *"whatever"* Craig had in mind, I moved into a studio and continued with life still searching for answers. I desired to make better decisions and the *"Craig incident"* left me in a quandary of feelings. I hoped that I would not make the same mistake again because next time I might not be so lucky.

In the process of self actualization, I desired to do some theater work to get my mind on something else. Needless to say, I was a *"terrible"* actress. I thought, let me do something that I have always wanted to do and since this was one of my passions as a child why not occupy time and explore my potentials. Unfortunately, in theater one can find trouble even if you don't look for it. It is no secret that in the theater, most often one could find other dysfunctional individuals. It was a community theater that Marvell's mother owned. This is where I met *"a preacher's"* kid named Allen. My heart was still yearning for a relationship and I thought that this good looking man, who was not only eloquent, articulate and a preacher, could be good for me. He invited me to church where his father was the Bishop. Within that same year, we began a relationship, I got baptized in his church— a non denominational *"Pentecostal/Baptist"* church, even though I still had issues with God.

Decisions, decisions and more bad decisions, Allen would sleep with me then criticize others about having sex before marriage and how he himself would not marry anyone that he had slept with. I can't believe it; he was just like my family a Cannibal Christian. He used the pulpit to hurt me and God knows who else he was doing this to at the time. Once again I journeyed into a place of confusion and anger. In 1997, I left that church and decided to move to downtown San Diego away from everyone. It was a very cute apartment; it was an old English flat.

I gave up on God and religion completely and began to exercise my gifts that had been spiritually handed down by my grandfather on dad's side and my grandmother Tita on my mother's side. They both practiced Santeria. Moving into my own place was a blessing. My quest to heal from past hurts was still flowing through my veins and it was in this apartment that I began to physically make changes, but without a God. I had the power to create my own destiny. Having my own apartment was an awesome experience it also gave me the opportunity to be on my own and working out some issues from my past that were tormenting me.

The only way I knew that I could begin to heal was to extract myself from my environment and from everyone. I took myself out of a destructive environment, and made my home conducive to my healing efforts.

Healing was extremely important for me, my life depended on it and I was not going to trust in a God that had let me down for so many years. My pursuit of happiness led me to a psychiatrist for therapy, I was open to anything. Unfortunately, the first thing the doctor wanted to do is place me on medication for my sleep deprivation. I did not agree with the psychiatrist because I knew that medication was a bandage and I found myself in bondage. I was ready to remove my bandages and break down the bondage. I was not a psychologist but I knew that I did not want a quick fix. I knew it was going to take time.

Do not get me wrong, I believe that medications can and do help many individuals however, our society has medicines for practically everything. It was my desire to heal from within and not depend on a bottle for my healing. I knew that I was not who I wanted to be because of so many years of others telling me who I was by others that were insane themselves. Why do I do the things that I do? Can I ever change? These were the questions that bombarded me day and night.

It seemed that at that time there weren't any psychologists that dealt with the kinds of issues I was experiencing. If there were psychologists around, I was not able to find them at that time. I recognized that I had a great deal of resentment, but I did not know how to get rid of the years of resentment and anger.

Times were difficult but I still pressed on in my healing process because I wanted to live. Some days I hated life and other days I was numb. There were days that I would cry myself to sleep and days that I could not function, I went through the motions and emotions. I was on the verge of breaking down in one aspect of my life, and in other areas of my life I was going through a breakthrough, all at the same time. I knew that I could not afford to have a breakdown so I pressed on. I made it a point not to allow myself to go through a breakdown, because suicidal thoughts began to surface again. I felt that I was so close, and yet so far. I did not want to die but I wanted life to stand still enough to catch up. I had to regain control of my life. Constant thoughts from my past haunted me. Sleeping was disturbed and so was my train of thought. For the first year in my process, I would often wake up sweating, with headaches and in physical pain. Anything could trigger an emotional outbreak. It could be a song, a sound, perfumes or hearing a little girl calling her mommy.

It is not my desire to self-diagnose, however, at the time; I believed that I was suffering from Post Traumatic Stress Disorder. The images of a woman being shot to death on television resonated in my mind over and over again. I believed everything that Walter told me even when he would say *"set a bird free, if it comes back it was yours, if it doesn't hunt it down and kill it."* There was a war inside my mind and I desired to break free. Anything could set me off; I was that fragile, watching television could send me off the deep end. I'd hear, on the television, that a child was kidnapped or a woman was assaulted and I would be a mess for days.

Trusting others was hard for me but then, on the other hand, I trusted too much. I was not balanced and this irritated me greatly. My thoughts dictated my life. Not many knew of my pain but those that I allowed inside would often tell me to get over it or that I was a mental case. Honestly, they were not too far from the truth. I knew how to mask my pain through laughter and clowning around. At times, I was told that it seemed that I had various personalities and yes they were right my coping mechanisms were to disguise myself like a chameleon. For each group I would surround myself with, I became a different person to appease the masses or to not be figured out. Only the wise were able to recognize that I was trying to satisfy everyone else and that it was breaking me mentally and emotionally.

One part of me wanted to die, and I would sound like Lisa, my aunt. Another part of me was very hypocritical and legalistic which made me sound like Mami. It seemed that for everyone who I had lived with that I became an extension of them. I did not know who I was, and I became who I disliked. Enough was enough; I had realized that I would not do things that I did not like to do just to appease others. I was trained to act like some of the most dysfunctional members of my family and I refused to be like them. I would rather die than to become like one of them.

Each day, I wrote in my journal and wrote letters to everyone, including mother and father but I never sent the letters out. Days would go by, and although I would be working and living my life, I would not finish a letter until I knew that I had really emptied my feelings. A letter could take one day to a whole week but still, it was not enough. I kept thinking that I could do more to really heal from my past hurts.

I decided to take a wicker chair that I had purchased from a local second-hand store and initiated a one sided conversation, voicing my pain. I made believe that the chair represented ALL my abusers. What compelled me to do this? I figured that I may never get a chance to speak directly to my abusers and I had to empty out my feelings towards them because it was killing me. Whatever I had in me, had to come out and since I could not speak to anyone, I took my chair, placed it in the middle of my living room and made believe that I was speaking to my abusers. I started journaling my emotions and feelings. I created a list of everyone that I could remember from as early as four years old to adulthood who caused me pain. I would talk to the chair, and for some individuals the talks lasted for several days. For some, like Mami, *"the candy man,"* Walter, and Edward, my talks lasted for months.

I would name the chair according to my abuser or the person I had issues with from my past. For some it took much longer than others. I would speak to the chair, yell, curse, and even hit it with a pillow. I would ask questions like why did they do what they did to me? Sometimes, I would kneel over the chair and cry, especially when it came to Mami.

For every breakthrough I would cry and feel at peace, but with Mami, it took a bit longer. It took a great deal to forgive Mami for asking me to lie all those years, then to use it against me. I was the *"scapegoat"* and like a fool, I willingly took part in this web of lies.

During my chair therapy and working on my issues with Mami, I was reminded of another time she betrayed me. It was October, 1987, right before my youngest daughter was born. I was visiting my family, who at the time lived in Yuma, Arizona. I was not feeling well and I had to leave my oldest daughter with Nelda as I stepped out. I told Nelda not to leave my daughter alone with Edward. Well, when I came back Edward went to grab my daughter to play with her and I blew up and told him to never ever touch my daughter. Well, the family got quiet and left it alone.

Rita became suspicious because of my reaction, not to mention that she was having an affair with a married man. She used this opportunity to confront me again. Apparently, Rita was having problems with Edward but I never knew it. Anyway, I was ready to leave their house when Rita called me into the room. I knew from the tone of her voice that she was going to ask me again. Before she even asked me, I told her *"yes, he raped me when I was a child,"* and then I walked away. This time, I was not going to lie for anyone anymore, so I said yes. Afterwards, Mami approached me and told me, *"You have ruined my daughter's life."* I was in shock! Mami wanted me to lie forever. She did not care about me and she confirmed it. Mami remained in my chair even longer than Edward the rapist.

During my healing process, life continued and of course, while dealing with issues from my past and placing my abusers on my living room chair, I found myself doing the same with recent offenders, but in this process, I learned to voice my feelings so that my chair was only used for past abusers.

This worked two-fold for me, by confronting my abusers from the past it allowed me to learn how to communicate my feelings to people in the present. I knew that my chair was still a chair and while I was speaking to the chair, voicing my pain and forgiving each one of the abusers brought me to a place, in my soul, where I experienced an unexplainable satisfaction and a sense of closure. There are no words to describe the feeling of being free, but when mental freedom is experienced, it is like Christmas in July.

The process of journaling and *"chair therapy"* took almost two years, but within those two years, my list was free from names. I was able to set boundaries, begin to love myself, and start thinking for myself—not like the rest of the family.

I learned that I could love a person, but I did not have to like them, their actions, or the way they behaved, because of who they were. For instance, I loved Mami, but I did not like her actions and how she handled situations. Placing boundaries was essential for my mental well-being. I did not have to accept what others perceived me to be, but rather who I perceived myself to be, therefore, I began to change my perception of myself and life.

I learned to love my kinky hair, my natural assets, my full lips, and myself as a whole. In fact, I am still a work in progress, but I love myself.

As for the chair, I do miss my chair and I wished that I would have kept it, but in a way, it's nice to know that the chair served its purpose. A chair is still truly a chair which made my house a home and finally, I learned to live and accept myself. Life is good! My question for you today is, can you honestly look in the mirror and see the beauty that God has created?

The Journey to Finding "Grace"

Chapter 12

When Love Finds You

"Love in its purest finds you when you are not looking. You do not have to fake it, make it or break it. It just flows gently into ones life and the past is forgotten." —VIVIONNE "GRACE" KELI

Anyone who knew Steven and me, knew that we were addicted to each other. In 1998, Steven and I rekindled our relationship. This relationship set me back a couple of steps. In my innate mind, I thought that I had invested too much into this relationship just to let it go. While still working on my healing process, I could not let go of Steven. He had asked me to move in with him in his Pasadena apartment early in the year. I looked for work and was hired toward the fall of 1998; I packed up my belongings, placed them in storage, and took a leap into the unknown. Things were not right from the start, but I kept working on me. I began to work for a big firm as an executive assistant to the vice president, and honestly, I do not know how I got that job because I was not at all qualified for the position. Incredibly, the ones that hired me knew that I was not qualified, yet they still offered me the position and I accepted.

It was here that I met Sangman, a real gentleman. Sangman became a strong foundation for me and although I reserved the right from trusting everyone, I chose carefully who I was going to trust. Things at home were real bad, Steven began to be rough with me, and we would argue up a storm. Believe me when I say this, Steven was my drug. As most people know, some relationships can be toxic, and ours was no exception.

Both women and men would call our house, leaving questionable messages, as if those weren't enough signs, I found sexually explicit videos of transvestites, but when I questioned Steven he gave me all kinds of excuses. It was his friend, he found them or they were given to him. Another incident was the day that a young lady called the house looking for Steven, she asked me who I was and I told her that I was one of Steven sisters visiting from out of town. She believed me and started telling me about their two-year relationship and how he was going to marry her. I asked this young lady about *"Grace"* his fiancée, what happened to her? She replied that he was living with her but she won't let him go. I cringed and kept my cool. Then I told her the truth and that I was Grace.

Steven found out that I had spoken to the *"other girl"* and begged me to marry him that evening so, we drove to Las Vegas, but I intentionally left my identification so we wouldn't be able to get married. I was no longer in love with him, but I loved him. I remember telling him many years earlier that, *"One day when I heal from my past hurts and begin to love myself, I will leave you."* That day was soon approaching. I pressed on to find out who I was and what kind of life I would have if I let go of people like him. We drove back to Pasadena, together and Steven started making arrangements so that we could get married. I could not see me getting married to Steven any longer. I loved myself and I wanted someone to love me, too. A couple of weeks passed, and Steven wanted to confess everything to me before we were married. He waited for the morning right before I went into work because he wanted to get it off his chest. He told me, *"I love you but I am interested in men as well."*

The shock did not hit me immediately. I said, *"Okay, I love you too. I will speak with you later after work."* I believe I was on the 110 freeway going through Pasadena when I realized what he had told me. Not only would I be in competition with women, but with men too? I could not think about this, I had to put my work face on and deal with it later. I drove into the parking lot at Olive Street in downtown Los Angeles; walked into an elevator full of people, including the vice president of the firm that I worked for. She asked me, *"Are you okay? You look pale. Are you okay?"* Then the elevator got very quiet. I looked straight into her eyes and said, *"Steven my fiancé told me that he is bisexual about an hour ago."* She said, "What!" She couldn't believe what he had told me that morning. The elevator was completely silent, and the vice president pulled me out on the next floor and we took the stairs.

She said, *"You won't be good for me today. Go home, and take care of your business."* I got back into my car and drove home and waited for Steven until he got home. When he arrived, we spoke, but honestly, I cannot recall the conversation. I could see him speak but I could not hear him, it's like I became deaf. All I knew was that I had to leave him. Suddenly, we broke out into an argument because he wanted me to speak with his father and I did not. He kept forcing me and finally, I got on the phone and told Steven's father about his son being bisexual. Steven was not happy, he grabbed the phone from me and gave his final good-byes *"dad, I am going to kill her and then kill myself."* When I heard this, I ran toward the door but he caught me, we wrestled to the ground and I managed to grab the phone and I dialed 911 but he took the phone from me. The 911 operator called back and he answered and told the operator that all was well but I yelled to come, they requested to speak with me and I did briefly. I told them that I was about to leave the house for good and gave the phone back to Steven, at which time I took the opportunity to get my purse and keys and leave while the 911 operator continued speaking to him.

Many blessings came after I left Steven. I finally said to myself, I love myself more than that now, and I will not be subjected to abuse any more. I learned that I can simply walk away and the world will not fall apart. It was during my time in Pasadena that I reunited with my family but mostly with Nelda. Nelda was on my list of forgiveness many years earlier as well, but for the first time, I was able to see her for who she was, a little girl in a woman's body trying to be an adult. Nelda became my friend and confidant. You see, forgiving Nelda allowed me to understand that I was not the only one suffering from my past hurts. I learned that others have suffered too and they also desire to change for the better. I realized how much of an amazing woman Nelda really was and I was blessed that she was in my life.

When I left Steven, I moved in with my father and Nelda.

Sangman started coming around my parent's home to visit me and began a great relationship with them. The blessings kept on coming, Nelda and I were like two teenagers and I continued to feel at peace. I remember once I told Nelda, while in my process of healing, that I was going to love her no matter what because I knew how she was raised. Now, she and I were like two peas in the pod.

Dad and I were also working things out, but disaster came once again. One day while living in dad's home, Nelda told me in secrecy that she wanted out of the relationship with my father. If she did not get out, she would kill herself. I helped her escape, unfortunately, sooner than later, the story of how and why things happen unravels faster than those involved would like. In this case, I was the accomplice aiding a friend to get away from dad.

When the family finally found out that I had helped Nelda, I was once again the family's biggest enemy. My love for Nelda was much stronger than the love I had for my own family because I knew Nelda and what she had endured her lifetime. I knew where she had come from and how tough her life with Dolores and Jose had been. So, when Nelda came to me, I decided to help no matter what others thought. Nelda left dad and went to live with Lily who had relocated to North Carolina several years earlier. At that moment, I believed sanity was more important than loyalty.

Dad, the family and I became estranged once again. Lisa the holier than thou, told me that I was less than garbage and that I was nothing. She told me that she hated me and told me right to my face, but I could not betray a friend, and Nelda was now truly a great friend. The power of forgiveness had catapulted my healing process and I was happy. Happy that on one hand, I was friends with my stepmother, yet sad that I lost the *"love"* of my family, which left me thinking, did my family really love me in the first place? I learned what true love was that year, and I embraced it and basked in it like a little child frolicking in a bed of flowers. It does not matter who loves me, but what really matters is that God loves me.

Love found me and I welcomed it. After the whole fiasco with dad and Nelda leaving, I went back to live in San Diego and stayed with Marvell until I got established but this time, I had hope for a brighter future.

The Road to Recovery

Chapter 13

Forgiveness Conquers All

"Forgiveness is . . . accepting God's sovereign use of people and situations to strip you of self importance, and humiliate your self love. —MARTHA KILPATRICK

Sangman became an intricate part of my life, and this time I learned the true meaning of love. You see, as long as I was with Steven, I was not opened to receive the kind of man I desired and needed. Once I released Steven, a good man came into my life and I was ready. I learned to appreciate him and love him like I have never loved anyone before. With Sangman, I learned how to communicate my feelings in a civil manner, without any repercussions. Sangman was always a loving person and through his love he taught me how to really have a relationship. As I was writing this chapter, I had to look back and laugh at myself because I was a savage... You could not believe the things that I put this man through and yet he showed me love and compassion. You see, physically, I was in my thirties but emotionally, I was still in my teens and it was my desire to catch up to my age.

Our relationship was clean and pure with no strings attached and it was an excellent feeling. He did not want me to change or to be something I did not want to be. He helped me during my family crisis. Sangman relocated to be near me and it was nice to meet someone who loved me enough by demonstrating it to me. Almost a year after we relocated to San Diego, we moved in with each other. Sangman was amazing; he wanted to make sure that I loved him so he waited another year to tell me that he was a millionaire. I was shocked! He showed me his portfolio and it was incredible, that he had all this money and yet lived a very simple life. This was also around the time that I met his mother.

In the Korean culture, the mother is highly regarded, because she is the matriarch. I was shaking because I did not know much about the Korean culture. I called a couple of my friends who are Korean and I told them that the time had come to finally meet Sangman's mother, what should I do? What do I say, how do I act? One of my friends told me that Korean mothers' prefer that their eldest son marry a Korean woman so be prepared for rejection. Oh my, that's not good. Another told me that if the Korean mother does not like me, I will never see Sangman again. I had nightmares that she was going to be a mean woman and she would dislike me.

The day arrived that I had the honor of meeting Mrs. Lee; we drove up the driveway to a very modest house. The lawn was perfectly manicured and she had a beautiful garden. I was extremely nervous but I had a feeling that Mrs. Lee couldn't be all that bad, after all, Sangman was a great man. When she came to the door, I was happy to see that she was smiling. She had a great disposition. She was a beautiful and classy woman. Mrs. Lee was no more than 100lbs, with wet clothes on, but she was so adorable in her mannerisms. She told Sangman, in her native tongue, that I was pretty and healthy. I asked Sangman, *"healthy?"* I found out that healthy, meant that I was still in childbearing years. I chuckled.

Mrs. Lee wanted to know more about my family and where they came from. Sangman explained to her that my parents are

Puerto Ricans from the island. She asked him what are Puerto Ricans and Sangman could not use anyone other than Jennifer Lopez. She gave me a puzzled look and quickly, I had to explain that not all Puerto Ricans are the same and maybe she might remember Rita Moreno or even Geraldo Rivera. She laughed! We had a fun time and I enjoyed her very much.

Dinner was excellent and it was time for us to leave. As I was leaving, Mrs. Lee told me something in Korean which in translation meant *"please come back."* We left and drove around the corner when Sangman began to get teary-eyed and I asked him, *"What did I do now?"* He stopped the car and said to me, *"You know, I can have many wives but only one mother."* I said, *"Okay."* Then he told me "if my mother did not like you, I could not marry you, but, she likes you so now we can get married." This was Sangman's way of proposing to me and I accepted.

In 2001, Sangman and I were married and have experienced many memorable moments. He has been my Rock of Gibraltar. My life seemed to be getting better and better. Sangman and I decided to invest a great deal of money into a corporation in La Jolla, California. We created a great business plan and were ready to begin when tragedy hit our great nation, on September 11, 2001, and set our project back. Loss of time equated to loss of funds. Each day that we fell behind in construction, our finances were depleted. It was costing us thousands per day. We couldn't stop the project because we had invested an exorbitant amount of money, up to this point. If we continued we were running the risk of overtaxing all our finances. We were between a rock and a hard place. If we stopped we were going to end up with nothing but if we continued we might lose everything as well.

I attempted to find ways to expedite our project but was not as successful as I had hoped. It was taking a toll on me and my husband. I began to develop different types of illnesses including sleep deprivation, in my life again, this time it was not Walter but finances. I also began experiencing strong supernatural occurrences.

Out of desperateness, I contacted my oldest cousin Nancy, who was now somewhat of a partner. I told Nancy of the occurrences that were happening, in my home, and asked for her opinion. To my surprise she referred me to her sister Sarah who happened to be a psychologist and her husband a psychiatrist as well. When I called Sarah our initial conversation was more about my dreams and the supernatural occurrence. She said she would get back to me. I had no idea that Sarah was a practicing Santera. Sarah requested that I fly to Miami, Florida, to meet her Santeria *"Godfather"* who was world-renowned.

I finally made it to Miami, Florida within a month, where I met the *"high priest"* the son of Shango, for advice about my dreams, supernatural occurrences and my business. He said, *"You are the daughter of no one."* I had no problems believing that because I truly believed that I was no one's child. Then he proceeded to tell me about my life and what I had gone through and that I must get a spiritual healing. My thoughts at the time were… since I am not God's daughter and since I was a bad child, that indeed, I must be no one's daughter. I was told that I needed protection from the Orisha's. The Santero stated, *"You must move out from where you are because an evil spirit has cast itself and there is no way to get him out but leaving."*

So, I returned to San Diego, CA and told my husband that we must move and we did within months. Within the same year and before I opened the business, I returned to Miami to get my spiritual cleansing from the Santero. Finally, I was free from evil spirits, so I thought, but that was not the case. In the new apartment, I began to see more apparitions and then I knew that there was an even bigger problem. Maybe, it is just me, and I am the one with the issues. In fact, there was a high profile kidnapping case at the time of my supernatural occurrences and one night while

I was sleeping the spirit of a little girl showed up in the corner of my room. I looked at my husband to see if he was awakened by the calling, but he was sound asleep. I remembered seeing this little girl once in a local store with her mother and then briefly on television, regarding her disappearance. The apparition kept on saying where I could find her body. Then she disappeared. I was devastated, and the next day I told my husband that I would like to go and find the little girl with the information that she had given me the previous night. However, Sangman absolutely refused. I also made mentioned of my dream to a young lady that I had befriended from a local television station and she said she would check up on it.

In the meantime, *"the Santero"* was scheduled to arrive, that very week, at my house and spend several days with us. Upon *"the priest's"* arrival, I mentioned my vision to him and what I had seen several nights before. That night, while we were watching television I saw some images on the television that looked like the images the little girl had described to me, and the "priest" said they found her body before they had even mentioned it on television. In a weird way, it felt as if a burden had been lifted off my shoulder. I got to thinking, maybe, the reason the god of my family did not help me when I was a child was because I was not his child but that of *"Shango."* This would explain my ability to have dreams, visions and the gift of communicating with the dead. And so it was... I embraced my new role in life in the occult.

Time was soon approaching, and I had to open my million dollar business. After many rituals and several flights back and forth for both the *"son of Shango"* and myself, my business was opened. The first year, we began to see profits as long as I made the spirits happy. We had to open up with a limited staff until we began to generate more income. It was nice to be a business owner and show off to my family that I wasn't so bad after all. Although I had forgiven them, what they thought still mattered. But the more I delved into the occult, the more I could care less what others thought of me, including my employees.

My powers in divination kept on improving but I was still missing something. The spirits would contact me at any time of the day, it became uncontrollable. In order to keep the spirits happy I had to do what they told me to do and it did not matter what time of day it was. The powers that were given to me were the ability to read tarot cards, be used as a medium, divination, and fortune telling. I was losing my mind because I could not tell what was real and what was not. During the day my business was a professional business but in the evening and once the employees left, I began my rituals, all the way into the morning, often with only a couple of hours of sleep. Sometimes, I had to ask an employee if they could see the person that was approaching me because spirits were known to materialize in front of me to give me messages from beyond the grave so, now I had to be conscious of who I was speaking to and sometimes my employees would tell me there was no one there, although I could see these *"spirits"* materialize.

It felt like I opened a spiritual portal that I could not close and became a slave to the spirits. These spirits did not leave me alone, they were constantly with me. I was running myself to the ground. I had become an evil and confused person. I was searching for something but I could not find it. My cousin Nancy who introduced me to Sarah, the sister in the occult, became worried for me and even brought a friend of hers, Bruni Quiñónez, to see if I would speak with her on other financial matters with the hopes that I would open up to her. The day that I met Bruni, the spirits were not happy and told me to stay away because she was a religious woman, who had other religious praying people such as herself. Not only were the spirits angry with me, but now I had a *"Christian woman"* along with other women, in Bruni's prayer group praying for me. There was one in particular that the spirits loathed and that was Dorothy Macey. Dorothy and Bruni were constantly praying for me, and the spirits could not handle it. I did not need their prayers. To keep the peace I stopped all communication with her. Then, I ran to another source of enlightenment.

As if I hadn't already learned my lesson, I then joined a *"new age"* movement with a big secret. But after much investment into this journey, of enlightenment, I learned a major lesson. If I desired to continue healing, I couldn't believe everything I heard.

I became tired of the *"new age"* movement and Santeria all together. I was physically and spiritually exhausted. Something was missing in my life and I could not place my finger on it. As if things weren't bad enough, my biological sister, Rachel's friend Debbie, called me on the cell phone to see if I would like to speak with my sister. I hadn't seen Rachel for almost twenty-two years. I told Debbie, that I would love to speak with my sister and we began communicating with each other. We wanted to see each other so I invited her to come to La Jolla, California, to see me. My only concern however, was that Rachel was also a Christian. I had my reservations about this Christian thing, but aside from that, I was excited and I truly desired to get my mind off of the business. While my sister acclimated herself to the beauty of La Jolla, she kept on mentioning God this and God that. Actually it was a bit annoying. The true reason that I was annoyed was that I could not understand how this God, that we both new and at one point loved, could protect her from sexual abuse and not me? I mean, here she was a woman in her thirties and she was still a virgin and untouched. Mother loved her and not us? I felt like Joseph's brothers and I hated feeling this way. I loved my sister but I couldn't help but question God.

The theme between Bruni and my sister was the same, God, God and more God. She would say the same things that Bruni kept mentioning to me and the spirits were not happy. I did not really want to hear it but I listened. During her stay, Rachel had a suggestion, *"let's go to Colorado?"* *"Colorado, what for"* I asked?

Well, apparently, her church was having a gathering with a large group of youth. I somewhat reluctantly, said, *"Yes,"* and the following month I met her in Denver Colorado. We arrived Friday and attended the first event. She introduced me to almost everyone she knew. Honestly, I was a little uncomfortable because I hadn't been around this many Christians in a long time. Not to mention, everyone knew my mother and insisted we were identical.

However, the scene was actually quite beautiful because there were many Christian children who seemed honored to be in attendance. Excitement was in the air. My sister and I stayed in the same room; I was stuck with her talking about the events and people that she would like to still introduce me to. After all, we had not seen each other for over twenty-two years. So we had much catching up to do. Saturday was full of events and there was a preacher who spoke about Rahab, the Prostitute, and it touched me greatly. Of course, the day would not be complete without Satan's minions, and I got to meet one face to face, she was a *"Christian"* but with a bad attitude and I was pleased to tell her that I was not a Christian and that I behave much better than she did, with her so called Christian attitude.

Aside from that incident, the day was spent well and now was coming to a close, when unexpectedly; I became very uneasy and uncomfortable. I could not place my finger on it until I glanced over and caught the eye of a young man. Immediately an inner voice said to me *"don't talk to that man"* or else, and so I turned the other way and proceeded to speak to my sister. To my surprise, the young man came over and introduced himself as Pastor Carl Rodriguez. What he asked me next was remarkable, *"how long have you been fighting them?"* I asked *"what?"* He repeated the question, and I asked this pastor to please leave me alone that I was advised not to speak with him and would rather keep the peace by obliging *"them"* I did not want to deal with *"them"* while I was there. *"I see that you are struggling with, some demonic forces,"* pastor Rodriguez continued. I explained that it is best that we just leave it alone, but he insisted, and *"they"* were not at all happy with the pastor. They wanted to hurt him by teaching him a lesson. That evening, he requested that we pray together and I was asked to meet him along with other pastors in the morning. Begrudgingly, I accepted.

My sister and I decided to retire for the evening, but what happened next astonished us both. I can't really recall, for it seemed that the night was patchy, with only vague memories of our conversation. I remember I couldn't sleep and I was mumbling about something to my sister. What I was saying to her, was the result of *"them"* not being happy with my sister, calling her stupid and such. As morning approached the conversation, with my sister, became more intense. As a result, my sister was not happy with me.

Sure enough, the time came to meet the pastors, and they came to our room and I was trembling and confused. All I can remember was entering the room and they began to pray. I was anointed and then I collapsed. After I came around, they continued to pray for me. For some strange reason I felt as though I was able to think clearly. I returned to La Jolla, California, and began to make some major decisions. Inner turmoil set in again do I begin a relationship with God or simply walk away for good? There was much confusion again. Everything was still the same but I was not. The business was facing the inevitable and there was no way to stop it. No positive mental thoughts, no spirits and no one could prevent the business from failing. One day out of pure desperation, I sat in my living room, listening to the ocean sway back and forth, and I started to speak, out loud, to God. *"If you really exist, you need to show me. I am not talking to just any god; I am talking to the God of Abraham, Isaac and Jacob. If you really exist you will need to show me and let me know who you really are. My tarot cards speak to me, the spirits led me and I have visions…but you have not shown me who you really are, I am not attempting to tempt you but the god of my family has never been there for me so my conclusion is that it could not be the same God of Israel. I do not know who you really are God, and it's been a long time since I have asked for help. Show yourself to me; let me know that you are listening. I am about to lose my business and health, not to mention my husband's investment."* As I opened up my heart and told God how I felt about Him and that I could forgive everyone else except Him, a peace entered me. I cried and begged for some sort of acknowledgement and within my spirit, a gentle voice unlike any other voice said, open the Bible to Matthew 6:28, and read. I was perplexed and asked *"what?"* Where am I going to find a Bible? Then I remembered that Nelda, my stepmother gave me a Bible the previous year, and I thought at that time, why would she do this?

I remember placing the Bible in one of the boxes so I frantically began to look for the Bible, thinking all along, what if there isn't a Matthew 6:28 at all and I am just wasting my time? But I pressed on, because my curiosity got the best of me and finally, I found the Bible. Now, the Bible was in my hand and I was trembling with joy and anxiousness because I thought again what if there isn't a (Matthew 6:28)? What if this is all a hoax? What if... Lastly, I opened the Bible with tears welling up in my eyes, hoping that God would not have led me on a wild goose chase. I was saying what will your Word do for me, am I about to lose everything I have worked so hard for?

Then I read the first verse:

So why do you worry about clothing? Consider the lilies of the field, how they grow: they neither toil nor spin; 29 and yet I say to you that even Solomon in all his glory was not arrayed like one of these. 30 Now if God so clothes the grass of the field, which today is, and tomorrow is thrown into the oven, will He not much more clothe you, O you of little faith?

31 "Therefore do not worry, saying, 'What shall we eat?' or 'What shall we drink?' or 'What shall we wear?' 32 For after all these things the Gentiles seek. For your heavenly Father knows that you need all these things. 33 But seek first the kingdom of God and His righteousness and all these things shall be added to you. (Matthew 6:28-33) NKJV

When I got to verse 33 and read *"but seek first the kingdom of God and His righteousness, and all these things shall be added to you."* I slammed the Bible shut and I stood very still. A fear entered my heart because only then was I able to see how deep into hell I had fallen. I couldn't believe that the Bible actually spoke. Why do I worry? I was so confused... I asked God to show Himself and now He did but how do I know it is not a fluke? That night, the demons were not at all happy and the torment was unbearable. *"How could you"* one demon would question? Where was your God when you were a child, another demon questioned? We will kill you and your daughters, we will kill your husband because we have given you power.

Several nights after I had opened my Bible the first time, I had a dream. I was dressed in white standing on the shore what seemed in front of a great multitude, they were standing in the water as if to be baptized. Apparently, I was speaking to these people at high noon. Then as the sun began to set, it stopped at mid point, then suddenly, out of nowhere, and without warning, a wave came upon this great multitude and swept more than 75% away leaving the other 25% still standing in the water. Then a voice from heaven said, "Many are called and few are chosen," then I woke up. "Many are called and few are chosen" I'd remembered hearing these words before but where and when? In my confusion, I still thought that I was meant to be a Santera, but the Bible stated otherwise.

This dream was very strange. I knew I needed to make the choice to follow Christ, but what did this dream mean? So instead of praying to God, I called "the priest" to find out what this dream meant. The priest said "a spirit is calling you and I will check to see what spirit is calling you; I will call you back." He was to find out which one of the Orisha's was calling me. I must say, it has been almost five years and he never returned my call. In time, I knew it was not the Orisha's calling me.

The spirits continued to torment me, threatening to kill me. They used the fact that, prior to conversion, my housekeeper died of a brain tumor, a personal friend was killed in Iraq, and my brother-in law was mysteriously killed in a car accident. They reminded me that things of this nature could happen to me or my daughters. I still pressed on, but now with God, I was not alone. I had had enough and decided to gather all my voodoo practicing materials: books, candles, incense, oils, tarot cards and videos, place them in my treasure chest and destroy them. I finally called Bruni Quiñónez and told her about my dreams and what I had decided to do with my life and she asked me to bring the items to her house and she emptied them in her trash can. I had surrendered all to this God of Abraham, Isaac and Jacob, who sent His only begotten Son to die on the cross for me.

Several weeks passed and I was scared to death to eliminate the last article of voodoo. Finally, through prayer I had enough courage to do what I was supposed to do with the remaining satanic items. While at my business I decided to get rid of an "elegua" a deity which I had hidden obscurely in a planter near the entrance of my business for blessings. I took the "elegua" and not only threw it into the dumpster; I smashed it so that no one would ever find it. I did not care to hear what the voices were saying any longer. I still pressed on. I was tired of being a slave to these spirits. My life was in turmoil, but I did not care. One by one, my employees left, or were terminated. I still pressed on, trying to figure out how to salvage my business. I wondered how the business could now be used for God and be blessed by Him. Some of my new Christian friends came to pray over the business and the property. By this time, I was really building a close relationship with God and it was my desire to do what He wanted me to do. After much prayer and seeking the scriptures, I asked God to bless me, my husband and our business. I was making a deal with God that if He allowed me to keep our business that it will be my mission to use this property for Him.

That night, I had another dream, this time I was in a big house and everyone in my family came to see me, when a voice said "look outside" and so I proceeded to go toward the big sliding doors, I opened the door and with my right foot first started to go outside but before I could get the other foot out the door a voice said "stop and look to your right" so I looked and I realized that my home was adjacent to a mausoleum. What did this all mean? As I continued to survey my house and the mausoleum half my body was outside and the other half was still inside and I could not move. In fact, as I studied the outside of the mausoleum, I also noticed that on the wall there was a plaque with the pictures of all four men that were buried there.

Suddenly, the images of these young men came to life, but they were demons who were now coming toward me, I could not move, I was trapped between being inside and outside and the only way I could find refuge from these demons was to enter my home, so, I fell back into the house where family members were able to pull me in completely and shut the door. When I awoke, I was still in my dream. I was dressed once again in a white robe and this time I had my hair wet. "How can I get out of this home?" I immediately got up and was looking for a way out. I entered into the library, the interiors were cherry wood finish, and there was a desk to the right hand side facing a big window directly to the left side. This window was approximately 17x17 and had no opening. As I stood in front of the window, I could see white tombs stones in formation, then I observed steps coming up to the big window with two white roman pillars on each side but no entrance or exit. Unexpectedly, I glanced back up to the white tomb stones. When I saw the dead rise from their graves they appeared to be normal, average looking people, not gory; I knew that these were the dead.

I then prayed "God, I do not wish to speak to demons anymore, I don't and I haven't since I accepted you, please make this stop." These demons continued to make their way to where I was standing but they never went up the steps. Some of these demons were saying "glory be to God" which confused me greatly. What caught my eye however, were two little girls that resembled me when I was six years old, they wore the same pigtails, uniforms and they even sounded like me. These twins had a satchel with them and they made the comment that in these satchels were the children that I had aborted in my youth. I rebuked them and broke down in tears.

"God please take me out of here;" but my dream continued and during this episode, I had several encounters with each one of the demons that I had seen at the beginning of my dream. The last encounter however, was vile and disturbing, because, it seemed that I was actually physically fighting a demon. I was not winning this fight and as I struggled with this demon, I cried out to God to release me, because it seemed as if I were fighting for my life. I was losing the battle, so it seemed, but I could not give up. So, I did the only thing I knew how to do, and that was to pray, "Please God save me." Suddenly, a very loud voice, unlike the gentle voice I had heard the first time said, "You have built your house on evil spirits and I will not bless your business. You will not lose your business but you won't keep it." Suddenly, I woke up, and then I realized what God meant. That same week, out of nowhere, a man came and asked if I was willing to sell the business? We sold the business and thus ended our journey in La Jolla.

Chapter 14

Finding the Treasure Within

"Give not that which is holy unto the dogs, neither cast ye your pearls before swine, lest they trample them under their feet, and turn again and rend you." MATTHEW 7:6 KJV

Did you know that we are treasures, sometimes hidden in the most obscure of places? Some of us are diamonds in the rough. Others are being refined through heat and will come out like fine gold. Some of us are being cultivated in slime and feces, locked up in a shell, only to manifest into fresh water pearls. Like any raw material, in order for us to become a spectacular gem, stone, or fine gold, we have to go through a process of resistance whether we choose to or not. Regardless of the circumstances that thrust you to go through this process, a key factor is time. It takes work to achieve the end result. We are ever evolving, but never the same. Each day, our form takes shape as we mature—a strand of silver to grace our hair today and tomorrow another; a touch of elegance lining our soft smiles and eyes, exhibiting the signs of time today and tomorrow. God made us special, a ballad of many notes that create a gentle lullaby of music, swaying to and fro.

The divine presence of God, the Conductor of our own inner musical ballads, should reign in our human essence as we are transformed. God's light must emanate through our eyes, illuminating the lost like that of a lighthouse guiding souls to God the "Rock of Ages." How beautiful is our Lord! The more we lean on the everlasting arms of Christ; we become transformed into His love and His image, which brings me to one of my favorite verses in the Bible. (Matthew 7:6) says it all—*"do not cast your pearls among swine."* If you are like me, giving of yourself blindly to please others only to feel used, you too have cast your pearls among swine.

Do you find yourself, giving all that you can give; have you depleted the love bank, making emotional withdrawals from your account so that others may love you more, respect you, maintain the peace? Do you keep giving your affection to confirm your love to another, or so that maybe they may appreciate you? Have you have bought these undeserving individuals off by bankrupting your emotional accounts; have you done all you can do, fought all you can fight, and still you end up alone, stripped away from your being, on the streets with nothing, physically or emotionally raped, and left for dead because you cared like Tamar? Who is Tamar?

There are many beautiful treasured stories in the Bible that I can empathize with. One is Tamar, second is Mary Magdalene and the last story although it took me a long time to understand is Job. Tamar's story starts like this, from (2 Samuel 13:1-22) NKJV:

> Now after this it was so that Absalom the son of David had a lovely sister, whose name was Tamar; and Amnon the son of David loved her. Amnon was so distressed over his sister, Tamar, that he became sick, for she was a virgin. And it was improper for Amnon to do anything to her. But Amnon had a friend whose name was Jonadab the son of Shimeah, David's brother. Now Jonadab was a very crafty man. And he said to him, "Why are you, the king's son, becoming thinner day after day? Will you not tell me?" And Amnon said to him, "I love Tamar, my brother Absalom's sister." So, Jonadab

said to him, "Lie down on your bed and pretend to be ill. And when your father comes to see you, say to him, 'Please let my sister Tamar come and give me food, and prepare the food in my sight, that I may see it and eat it from her hand." Then Amnon lay down and pretended to be ill; and when the king came to see him, Amnon said to the king, "Please let Tamar my sister come and make a couple of cakes for me in my sight, that I may eat from her hand."

And David sent home to Tamar, saying, "Now go to your brother Amnon's house, and prepare food for him." So Tamar went to her brother, Amnon's, house and he was lying down. Then she took flour and kneaded it, made cakes in his sight, and baked the cakes. And she took the pan and placed them out before him, but he refused to eat. Then Amnon said, Have everyone go out from me. "And they all went out from him. Then Amnon said to Tamar, "Bring the food into the bedroom that I may eat from your hand." And Tamar took the cakes, which she had made, and brought them to Amnon her brother in the bedroom. Now when she had brought them to him to eat, he took hold of her and said to her "Come, lie with me, my sister. And she answered him, "No, my brother, do not force me, for no such things should be done in Israel. Do not do this disgraceful thing! "And, where could I take my shame? And as for you, you would be like one of the fools in Israel. Now therefore, please speak to the king; for he will not withhold me from you."

However, he would not heed her voice; and being stronger than she, he forced her and lay with her. Then Amnon hated her exceedingly, so that the hatred with which he hated her was greater than the love with which he had loved her. And Amnon said to her, "Arise, be gone!" And she said to him, "No, indeed! This evil of sending me away is worse than the other that you did to me." But he would not listen to her. Then he called his servant who attended him, and said, "Here! Put this woman out, away from me, and bolt the door behind her." Now she had on a robe of many colors, for the king's virgin daughters wore such apparel. And his servant put her out and bolted the door behind her. Then Tamar put ashes on her head, and tore her robe of many colors that was on her, and laid her hand on her head and went away crying bitterly And Absalom her brother said to her, "Has Amnon your brother been with you? But now hold your peace, my sister. He is your brother; do not take this thing to heart" So Tamar remained desolate in her brother Absalom's house But when King David heard of all these things, he was very angry. And Absalom spoke to his brother Amnon neither good nor bad. Absalom hated Amnon, because he had forced his sister Tamar.

Why this story? This story touches a lot of women throughout the world. At some time or another, many have trusted someone in their lives, only to become a modern day Tamar. Amnon was a predator preying on the innocent. Amnon committed premeditated assault on a living person that was offering her kindness, her love and her compassion to him. A person who was raped then discarded like trash. This precious treasure was made into a trinket, but what was interesting to me is the fact that Absalom realized what had happened and told Tamar, "Hold your peace, my sister. He is your brother; do not take this thing to heart."

Basically, forgive and release, for Amnon is your brother, like so many brothers in our lives that have done the same in different capacities. The woman was violated, stripped of her virginity and her opportunities. How many of you can sense her pain? I know I can. At first, I really got upset with Absalom for taking it so lightly. Then I started thinking well, he's a man! He doesn't understand this inner turmoil of the female psyche. But in the context of this book, he is right. We who have experienced abuse no matter how awful it may be we must hold onto our peace!!! In essence, he was saying, "Do not cast your pearls among the swine," what is done is done.

Amnon was a swine who robbed Tamar of her innocence. Tamar did not have a choice in her time. We, as women, have more choices today, and I thank God for that. Too often, females of all ages are abused physically, mentally, emotionally, sexually, and spiritually. Tamar knew she was a treasure for she knew that she was a virgin, but that was taken from her. How well do you value yourself? Even though you may or may not have experienced the same in your life, have you held your peace with other issues in your life? Holding your peace does not mean staying quiet, but rather it is about speaking up while allowing God to fight your battles.[2] So often, our peace is surrendered to individuals that could care less if we were to drop dead. Knowing that you can still speak and maintain your peace is vital to your spiritual growth. God said it to the Israelites, *"God will fight our battles and ye shall hold your peace"* (Exodus14:14) NKJV. Whether you give of yourself willingly or unwillingly, you lose a part of yourself physically, mentally, emotionally, and/or spiritually to a non-deserving individual, and when you have done this, you are actually casting your pearls among the swine. *"Do not give what is holy to the dogs; nor cast your pearls before swine, lest they trample them under their feet, and turn and tear your pieces"* (Matthew 7:6) NKJV.

Do you sometimes wonder why you are struggling with a certain person or situations? Maybe the reason for the struggle is because at times, we must learn from the person or situation, which I strongly believe is the process of refining. Remember, God told us that we will suffer,[3] but that does not mean that we must give up on life. Let me further illustrate how Satan desires to destroy your connection with God. I want you to look at yourself and consider yourself as God's wonderful treasure, *"thus says the Lord, Now if you obey me fully and keep my covenant, then out of all nations you will be my treasured possession. Although the whole earth is mine"* (Exodus 19:5) NKJV

Now let us consider all your gifts/treasures that God has given you (e.g., singing abilities, speaking abilities, healing, prayer, loving, and such) each individual gift is a pearl, a diamond, or a ruby, and you are the vessel holding these wonderful treasures—a treasure within a treasure. Let us say that God is blessing you abundantly, and you are basking in His light when Satan comes in, as he always does, and places an Amnon character in your life. Please keep in mind that Amnon characters can be female or male, young and old. If you allow this Amnon character to control your emotions and your thoughts keeping you away from your time with God then Satan has won the battle. His scheme has been accomplished because Satan's Amnon has led you away from God and if you do not forgive this Amnon then you have opened up a portal to resentment and anger. What you have done is that you have allowed Satan to rob you of your treasures. How will Satan rob you of your treasures? If you do not forgive, you will find yourself being lured by Satan through anger, which makes you lose your devotion, praises, your adoration and your focus on God. Tamar could have killed Amnon or possibly taken her own life, but she went on her way and was told to hold her peace. Whatever you have endured in your lifetime, you must see that you are not alone and it is not your fault. Granted, sometimes, because of our past, we do not know how to set boundaries and can place ourselves in vulnerable situations to be victimized. However, most often than not, we must understand that Satan will use everything in his arsenal and we must be cognitive of our feelings, emotions and mental processes to understand that our battle is not only with flesh and blood, but more so with principalities. Realizing that God has so much for you will allow you to understand that you have become a warrior. Let us face it, we have invested time, money, our hearts, and, for some people, our very own lives for someone or something that is not worthy of, our emotions, our love or our pearls. You are God's special gift and treasure to be used for the edification of the God who created us.

As you may recall, at age eight, I trusted my Uncle Edward. Along with what happened, came confusion, self-hate, anxiety, doubtfulness, anger, hurt, feelings of being unworthy, and loneliness. I created an impregnable jail cell and I made sure that no one could enter in mentally, but physically I had no power. It took me a long time to forgive Edward and Mami because they treated me as if I was the bad person. They molded me then hated me.

As you recall in the chapter "A Chair is Still a Chair," between 1996 through November 1998—I declared a war on my mind. I would sit in my living room and speak to a chair. I made believe that this chair was representing the individuals that caused me great pain during my childhood. I would tell the chair how I felt. I cried and I screamed, and each time, I allowed myself to forgive. The more I forgave, the more I changed the way I thought about the world and the faster the healing came.

Can you ever trust again? After one has been violated, it is hard to confide or trust anyone. The tendency is to believe that everyone is out to get you, and it may be true for some people. Generally, not everyone is out to get you, but at times, it can feel that way. Please do not close your mind to receive God's word or withdraw from God, for His love is ever so pressing. I pray that you are able to understand how changing your thoughts can lead to a better tomorrow. Also, keep in mind that what helped in my healing process, may not work for some and vice versa.

I know that my peace of mind has been restored and when I feel that my peace is being compromised I find ways to maintain my peace by walking away from an issue for a moment, reading a book, or even taking a drive. Please do not stop living because someone decided to take advantage of you. Do not stop edifying

God because your pearls were trampled upon. Your testimony and your experiences may help others understand the power of forgiveness. God has given you gifts. Are you going to stop singing because that person goes to the same church? Are you going to stop fellowshipping, witnessing, caring, writing, living, and enjoying life because an Amnon caused you pain and is around you and the people that you know? If so, then you are casting your pearls among swine. Do not stop showing your true beauty, because some person or persons did not know how to treat a precious treasure. Healing starts now; it starts with you!

Get in the habit of claiming the promises. I am God's treasure, and although Satan wanted to make me out to be a cheap trinket, my God has given me a crown of glory and I will serve Him. I choose this day whom I will serve. Know that whatever gifts you have received they are irrevocable. *"For the gifts and the calling of God are irrevocable"* (Romans 11:29) NKJV.

Are you willing to open your jail cell that you have created in order to protect yourself from your past and the demons that accuse you or keep you from others and possibly even God? Trust me, you are not alone. You have the key in your heart, deep down inside where you have not looked for such a long time.

In order to be able to fight your demons, you must be in prayer, and in the Word put on your armor each day found in (Ephesians 6:11-13) NKJV

Put on the whole armor of God, that you may be able to stand against the wiles of the devil. For we do not wrestle against flesh and blood, but against principalities, against powers, against the rulers of the darkness of this age, against spiritual hosts of wickedness in the heavenly places. Therefore take up the whole armor of God that you may be able to withstand in the evil day, and having done all, to stand.

Also, it is best to know who your enemy really is... he is Satan but most important it will behoove you to know who you are in Christ. Please keep in mind that the victory has been won at the cross through our Lord and Savior Jesus Christ, so we are not fighting to win the victory but to keep the victory. This process does not happen overnight, but rather systematically. Now find the sword in this case, your Bible that is, if you have one, take it out, and dust it off. Break through your first door, the door symbolizes your mind. There will be some inner resistance, but remember who you are in Christ. It will be hard to push, but use the tools empowered by Christ to push this door open and begin to heal.

Remember, the battle is for your mind; therefore, use your weapons to break through your first door. At first, things will be dim, as you go through the door. Your eyes will try to adjust spiritually. Ask God to walk with you; His word will be a lamp unto your feet and a light unto your path.[4]

In this process, you will begin to understand God's will for you. Listen to the scriptures and learn the voice of God, for He has special things awaiting you. Do you know that God is waiting and has been waiting for this moment? God says, in (Isaiah 41:10) *"Fear not, for I am with you; be not dismayed, for I am your God. I will strengthen you, Yes, I will help you, I will uphold you with My righteous right hand."* However, not only is God saying, *"Fear not,"* He makes sure that you understand that you are loved and those who caused you pain will pay the price. *"Behold, all those who were incensed against you shall be ashamed and disgraced; they shall be as nothing. And those who strive with you shall perish"* (Isaiah 41:11) NKJV.

After I reconciled with the Lord, got baptized, developed a strong prayer line with Christ, and began to build a close relationship with Him, Christ had me ready for my first mission. In the winter of 2004, God made it possible to obtain a job in Sacramento, California, as a marketing consultant. I was praying to God to give me my first real assignment now that I was armed and ready for battle. Within weeks, I was making friends as I always do. My walk with the Lord was strong and I desired to find out my mission, but in the meantime, I occupied my time. During my prayer, I was inspired to sing in a band, so I approached one of the guys that worked on the floor and asked him if he knew of a Christian band with which I could record a CD. He gave me a puzzled look and stated that he was the drummer for a Christian band. I found that odd, but I knew that God was inspiring me to ask him. I proceeded to ask him if he knew of a place where I could volunteer, such as a homeless shelter. He laughed and said, "My band plays at the local homeless shelter." I asked God, "Okay, where is this going?"

He invited me to go the following Saturday to hear them play during practice, but something happened and he asked if I could come on Sunday's worship instead, I agreed. Sunday morning came, and although I was very tired. God's voice was leading me to get up and go. After arguing with him for about 30 minutes, I said, *"Alright I will go, but I do not like this one bit."* I showered, got dressed, and headed to the homeless shelter. I got there in time for the band to begin praise and worship. I made eye contact with the drummer and I sat down, all angry and not understanding why God had me there when He knew that I was extremely tired. I tried to bargain with God that any other day would be okay with me.

My thoughts at the time were, 'What is the purpose?' I sat next to individuals that were hygienically challenged, and I began to complain to God. His response was "I came to die for these people too." Wow! This hit me like a rock, so I began to praise Him. Then again I began to question God, and in a tantrum mode, I asked God, what was His purpose for me being there? There was nothing that I could possibly learn from this homeless shelter. I had a great marketing opportunity and my husband was working, so why was I there? By the time I finished asking why I was there, a young woman had caught my eye. I knew her. I told God, "That is not fair." What was I supposed to do now? I began to cry and I had to get up and step away.

A counselor from the shelter came and she asked me if I was okay. I responded to her, saying, *"God wanted me here today and I almost missed the opportunity to meet someone that I have not seen for a very long time."* She asked me, who was the person that I supposedly had known? I said, *"That young lady dressed in pink and in jeans,"* and I pointed to the young woman. Then she told me that the young woman had lived in the lobby on and off for about two years and they did not know of anyone that might know her. I said I know her, *"I remember when they brought her home from the hospital as a newborn—she is my first cousin. I have not known her whereabouts for over sixteen years, and now I find her here."*

I requested that they not let her know that I was there and for her to listen to the spiritual message that God had for both of us. God confirmed my visit by having the preacher speak on forgiveness. After the service, I went up to my cousin and called her by her name. She recognized me and I asked her why was she there. She stated that she had been homeless for a while. I continued talking to her and noticed that she was struggling with some demonic forces. I asked her by the power of Jesus Christ tell me what demons was she dealing with, and she began to name them—the demon of fear, the demon of confusion, the demon of resentment, and the demon of schizophrenia so forth and so on. I demand them to depart, but I knew that I could not do it in one moment, so I began to work with her and set guidelines, boundaries, and I gave her a Bible to read. I had a strategic plan to combat these demons through intercessory prayer and supplication for her soul.

Please understand that this could not have been at all possible without the power of our Lord, Jesus Christ. The power of forgiveness, prayer, fasting, and obedience, along with the armor of God, is given to everyone. This process was not a quick fix, it took me three months. On the third month, once she began the road to recovery, she called me to tell me that she was thankful that I came into her life and that I saved her life. I did nothing of the sort; I just focused on my mission. I had to be disciplined in the Word, not to give into her stories, not to waiver and not to lose hope for myself or her. Also, my job began to take a downward spiral, and I chose to resign. God was telling me, your job here is done.

I am glad to report that my cousin has been off the streets and in her apartment for over four years and she is going to church. She is still a work in progress but only she can go to Christ and confess her inner most secrets and pain. She is still on the road to recovery but this time, she is not alone, she is with Christ. Without surrendering to the fact that she needed help and intervention, her healing could not begin. I fulfilled my mission and was heading back home to be with my husband.

My question to you today is what is your testimony, how has God pulled you through and how can you help others?

Chapter 15

Finding Life on "Root 66"

"I'd rather be rebuked into Heaven, than loved into hell."

—VIVIONNE "GRACE" KELI

In the early part of 2004, I made a conscious decision to know God and understand His mercies, because of my horrific childhood, I could not understand who God was, and what role would He play in my life. God confirmed my mission while I was in Sacramento helping my cousin. As I returned back from Sacramento, I was baptized into God's family in the spring of 2005 with my husband, Bruni, Dorothy and dad at my side. You see, what I learned about God was that He allowed me to live, breathe, and to understand that those who did wrong to me were now in God's hands.

Friend, as I stated in this book from the beginning, you may or might not have gone through what I have gone through, but if you are reading this book, chances are that you or someone you know have suffered and find yourself questioning God, I need you to understand that you are not alone. By now, you should realize that forgiveness is vital for true recovery. Hopefully, by reading this book, it will unleash the after effects of abuse so that recovery can begin as it did with me. In the Bible, Jesus was asked, how many times should one forgive? Jesus responded 70 x 7. (Matthew 18:21-22) NKJV:

"Then Peter came to Him and said, "Lord, how often shall my brother sin against me, and I forgive him? Up to seven times?" Jesus said to him, "I do not say to you, up to seven times, but up to seventy times seven." That does not mean that we should take our clicker and count how many times we forgive; it just means that we must keep forgiving.

In the Bible, it also states that even Jesus, while still on the cross, asked His Father to forgive us—*"for they do not know what they do."* (Luke 23:34) NKJV. How did Jesus ask for forgiveness? He prayed His last prayer.

As you read about my childhood crisis, my prayers seemed to have been unanswered and in vain, but I now understand that God knew what I could handle. It is written in (John 16:33) NKJV *"These things I have spoken to you, that in Me you may have peace. In the world you will have tribulations; but be of good cheer, I have overcome the world."*

God knows your pain and He too is in pain, for He loves us, but He cannot make someone be good if he or she is not willing to be good. All the abusers and molesters in my life were not good people, no matter what position they held in the church, how good they could sing in the choir, or even how much money they made.

The hardest lesson for me was when I came to the realization that no matter how much they hurt me, I had to forgive. Please hear me out. When you forgive, you release these individuals from your mind into God's possession. Only He can take vengeance on these people, not us. Once you forgive, you will receive peace of mind. I know firsthand. Let God do His work and let your abuser deal with God. After all, it is between God and them.

Remember, I did not come back to Christ until 2004, so everyone that I had forgiven was through enlightenment and new age thinking, but something was still missing. I strongly believe that my growth was not complete because I had not reconciled with God. It was not easy at first, but my prayer began with, *"Lord, help me to get control of my mind and help me to capture my thoughts."* It was my desire to be free from this self-inflicted prison cell, which I had created for myself in my mind.

The lesson that I valued the most, was, that I could hate the sin, but love the sinner and we all are sinners in the eyes of God [1]. I realized that with God, every thought I had of each person in the past or in the present, could be controlled through Christ because my mind was in Him. [2]

Since God touched my heart, I am no longer a slave to my past. I have become a warrior for Christ, helping other women and men to understand that they are not alone and that they too can help stop sexual abuses on children in and outside the church. It is a battle.

Do you know whom you are fighting? It is written, *"For we do not wrestle against flesh and blood, but against principalities, against powers, against the rulers of the darkness of this age, against spiritual hosts of wickedness in the heavenly places"* (Ephesians 6:12) NKJV. Like any war, we must know our enemies to be better prepared to fight the battle. Who do you think was behind the monstrosities that you endured as a child or even as an adult? To best answer this question, you must first acknowledge that there is a being called Satan, that is the only way to fighting this battle.

Believe it or not, prayer and knowledge of the Word are the first keys to true recovery. Get rooted in all sixty-six books of the Bible. That's the real Root 66! Prayer is the constant communication between you and God. Whether you are kneeling, lying down, or making a quick mental thought, it is still a communication with God; building a relationship is important. Learn who God is and why He is God. For those who have been molested by their fathers, it may be difficult to see God as a loving father. If this is the case, then see God as a loving King and an advocate for you. You must be willing to choose on whose side you are going to be. There is no such thing as being in the middle. Choosing whom you will serve will determine the outcome of your recovery.

In Matthew 6:24 NKJV, Jesus says, *"No one can serve two masters, for either he will hate the one and love the other, or else he will be loyal to the one and despise the other. You cannot serve God and mammon."* As a warrior by default, you cannot be in both camps. Remember that Satan will use anything in his arsenal to attack you, no matter what age you are. You must stand firm and know who you are in Christ. It was difficult for me to identify myself in Christ. I had to train myself to believe and affirm this noble position, because as a survivor, I had to take care of myself. Knowing who I am in Christ has allowed me to let go of the idea of trying to take care of myself. God has given me the strength to withstand many battles since I have accepted Him into my life as my Savior. As a warrior, my allegiance is with God.

Let me tell you how God really works, you read about my cousin's healing which started in the winter of 2004 through January 2005 and what a positive experience that was however, prior to my cousin's experience, the first real God experience testing my faith was when, for the second time in my life, I went to visit mother.

The first day that we met, it was unbelievable how much I looked like mother. We settled in for the evening however, mother came into my sister's room and told me to *"please lock your door; I wouldn't want anything to happen to you."* I thought that was a bit odd but I did what I was told.

The next day, mother and I spent time together talking about my past again but because of my last experience with her, I kept quiet and talked about other things. She did try to find out about dad and his wife and well, I was vague about his dealings. Well, the third day, Rachel wanted me to go with her to work and hang out so, I left my address label along with other work related information on the bed. Something told me to put them away but, I ignored it. Well, we came home early that night and I spoke with mother a little bit more and she began talk about dad and how cruel he was to her, I told her that she should forget about the past and live life. There are so many beautiful things out in the world to explore and she and Rachel should go and check them out. I also mentioned to mother that even Jesus suffered, and if He suffered why should we be exempt? Well, mother told me that God knows the truth and how much she has suffered and that she does not have to forgive. Well, I said, *"if you want to believe that, then there is nothing that I can do for you."*

Mother then went into her old self again and told me that she only had one daughter and she only loves one daughter. I told her, *"Listen to yourself; you gave birth to me as well. How do you expect me to respond to that statement?"* She gave me a disturbing look and said, *"I don't know what you mean."* I asked her, did you give birth to me? She could not reply.

It was about 10:00 PM that evening, and I retired to my room. I gave her a kiss goodnight and left it alone. I did not go there to prove anything but only to see mother and Rachel. During the early morning, God stepped in and woke me up at 4:00 A.M., I was told to get on my knees and pray, as I would be leaving mother's house soon. I was also told that there was a lesson in all of this that I had to learn. I argued with God and told Him that I would like to stay, but He continued to press on for me to pray and so I did. I finished praying around 6:00 A.M., and was told to pack my luggage because I would be leaving mother's house that morning. Reluctantly, I did what I was told. I got dressed and as I stepped out of the bedroom, I realized that my mother's voice had changed and that she was cursing and was very anxious. The other entity was emerging like when I was a little girl and my first instinct was to hide under the bed for a brief moment. She was not the same woman I had been speaking with for the past few days. Her demeanor and even the sound of her voice had completely changed. I asked if she was okay, but she ignored me, so, I went to my sister and stepfather and told them that I would be leaving for good.

Unfortunately, Rachel went to mother to complain that she did not want me to leave and mother became furious with me. Mother opened her mouth and began to abuse me verbally. She said the vilest things to me and told me, *"I hope you die. I hope that your airplane crashes. I hate you, I will never bless you."* I realized the lesson that I had to learn at that moment. I remember hearing a little voice saying, *"I am the Lord, your God, and I bless you."* [3] I looked at my mother and I told her in a gentle voice, *"Mother be careful of whom you serve, for at the time of your death, it may not be God that you see."* In an instant, she started looking for a butcher knife but could not find it in her regular spot. I gathered my belongings and was heading toward the door. Mother was fast approaching me and I told her, *"Stop in the name of Jesus Christ, my Savior. I demand to speak to the demon that has my mother."* She stopped and turned pale like snow, and looked at me, and with a gentle, calm, and sweet voice said *"please leave before something happens to you."* Only then, I realized that I was speaking to my mother for the first time in my life and not to her demons. I would not have been able to confront my mother's demon if I was not prepared in prayer.

Satan tried to use everything in his power to destroy me that day, because I had chosen my Savior Jesus Christ and I was victorious. And although, I was left with the question as to "Why" all, I could figure out was that when I get to heaven I will have the opportunity to ask God. In the meantime, I would not be caught up in wondering about why's, but I would occupy my time by reaching others and praying for the recovery of everyone I encounter.

Once you begin to build a relationship with God you have power—the power to do all things (Philippians 4:13) NKJV. *"I can do all things through Christ who strengthens me but you must believe this."*

Chapter 16

Becoming an Effective Warrior

"I can do all things through Christ Jesus which strengthens me."

PHILIPPIANS 4:11 NKJV

"I knew I could do all things through Christ" including becoming a warrior for the greater good. If you have suffered great pain and losses as a child and even as an adult and you are still here breathing—then you are a warrior. I never wished to become a warrior for Christ because I knew that warriors had to fight in battles regardless of what side you are on and I did not want to fight. However, the many things that thrust us into a war can be mental, physical and even spiritual and in essence, we will always be in the battle, the question is whose battle Christ or Satan's?

We are in a war together and we should all stand firm in unity and together we can fight our inner wars. I need you as much as you need me to fight the enemy. I am a survivor and I am alive which by default, makes me either a child of God or the enemy. When I chose Christ, I automatically became a warrior who survived my past. You see, I had to choose between God and or Satan. Now, please hear me out, we are in a spiritual warfare and everyone is involved. I am not talking just about religious wars, but rather talking to you about the real battlefield that is going on in this world today for your very soul. Great and horrific crimes are being played out on humanity. As long as we breathe, we are survivors of some sort of war. You have great warriors and not so great warriors.

Do we have a warrior's manual? Yes! Indeed. How do you become an effective warrior and where do you get your gear for the battle? As you read in my previous chapters, I was in a war when I had my business to keep the "spirits" happy, but they made me into a slave. When I decided to leave the occult, I was in a new war zone, praise God that now I was an enemy of Satan. In the early parts of my true conversion in 2004, I was tormented by demons and during the night I would be awakened abruptly by demons telling me that they were going to kill me. The more they harassed me, the more I had to read the Word. My mind would be attacked while driving; I would suddenly forget how to drive confusing the brake with the gas.

The war was on. I knew that when I chose God I would enter into a war but I never knew to what extent. Nothing prepared me for this war but I knew that I was in it and that if I walked away now I would surely die. I wondered how I could become a warrior and fight but I could not find all the answers.

It was scary to know that I had a death warrant on my head because of the choice I made. Clearly the enemy was not about to give me up that easily but I knew that I could not give in. I had to avoid certain movies, television shows that dealt with witchcraft, secular music, especially sexually explicit literature, and even images. In fact, I went as far as to completely stop visiting a local amusement park that focuses only on "magic" because I was going cold turkey.

Witchcraft is intoxicating and if the mind is weak, Satan can overtake the person. I am not sure if I can explain what I went through but it was a withdrawal and it was very bad. Witchcraft is addicting and I chose to surrender it all. Some days, I would hear, come back to us. Other days, someone at church would do something that left me broken and the spirits would say *"see, Christians are not all that good, come back, you know where you belong, you have power with us."*

The more I heard the "spirits" the more I had to get into the Word. The airwaves are filled with demonic influences and it did not matter where I went, something or someone would try to entice me to come back to the spirits. Many things happened throughout my conversion to Christ but I knew that I had to remain in the battlefield. I had to test all things... Unfortunately, or fortunately, I had a sense of discernment when I met a person; I knew that either they were practicing or fighting demons. God is so good that now even when visiting some churches, God has given me the ability to know when people are struggling with the occult or demonic forces.

Each time, Satan presented a spiritual battle I got deeper into the Word. Why? Because we are in a spiritual battle, our gear is not physical apparel, but rather a spiritual armor. It is written, *"Finally, my brethren, be strong in the Lord and in the power of His might. Put on the whole armor of God that you may be able to stand against the wiles of the Satan"* (Ephesians 6:10). As warriors, we must put on armor every day. There are seven steps to this process. The steps are written in Ephesians 6:14-18,

> Stand therefore, Having **girded** your waist with truth Having put on the **breastplate** of righteousness Having **shod** your feet with the preparation of the gospel of peace Above all taking the **shield** of faith with which you will be able to quench all the fiery darts of the wicked one. And take the **helmet** of salvation, and the sword of the Spirit which is the world of God; **Praying** always with all prayer and supplication in the Spirit, being watchful to this end with all perseverance and supplication for all the saints.

In any war, whether it is spiritual and or physical, there will be casualties. Some will lose limbs, and even their lives; however, our armor prepares us, spiritually, to be on alert, and when the time comes for our war to be finished on this earth, our battle would not have been in vain.

We must remember that our minds are in constant war with the enemy. Most of the battle between God and Satan is for the possession of our mind, body and soul. That is why Satan continues to use our past; it's the strongest tactic he can use against us. He uses our past to control us, if he succeeds in trapping us with our past experiences and pain, then he has won the battle. The battle of the mind is real and detrimental to our wholeness. Prayer is a constant communication with our heavenly Father and King, to keep us on the right track. He might not answer immediately, but He always does. I stress again and again, along with prayer, survivors should get to know the Word.

In order for me to effectively fight Satan, I have to be able to use my sword (the Word) because that is my ammunition. Becoming knowledgeable, reading the Word each day, and learning verses will give you ammunition when the time comes to combat Satan. Just recently, I was in a situation in which I had to fight with a demon that was trying to destroy someone that I knew.

How important was my sword to me? I remembered that I had given my Bible (sword) to a sister in church, who was to refurbish it; so, I used another Bible that I was not accustomed to using. Basically, this Bible was not "broken in" like my older Bible. It was a bit awkward because I was used to pulling out my Faithful Sword and easily finding scriptures. I had to fight this demon with what I could remember.

The battle lasted about forty minutes. You see, there was a friend that came to me and gave me some pills because she was afraid to take her life but something was pushing her to end her life. When I walked into her bathroom which was adjacent to her master bedroom, something told me to go into her bedroom. Sure enough, there was a demonic force over her bed and the room was ice cold. I grabbed my newest Bible but I could not find my passages.

Most of my favorite passages were marked in my older Bible and I had to reach into the index of my mind to retrieve what I knew. I fought this demon and he came back with accusations and condemnation. Now, let us think about this for a moment, if I had not been prepared, what do you think would have been the outcome?

You cannot retrieve something you never had, and if you've never had the Word rooted in your mind, how can you fight against Satan? What I remember about this battle is one question that the demon kept asking me, "Who are you?" I had to tell him that I was a daughter of Jesus Christ. He kept asking under what authority I came to him. I told him that I came under the banner of my Lord, Jesus Christ who shed His blood for me on Calvary's cross. He began to remind me of my past sins, as well as my present sins. I told him, "My sins are forgiven, thus says the Lord, my God, and they are cast in the bottom of the ocean. And as for sins that I am not aware of, I come to the foot of the cross now and confess them." My friend saw all this, and threw herself on her knees. She began praying for her life. That night she could have perished. Unfortunately, as the demon left, we did not notice that the female dog in the room ended up becoming an evil dog overnight which then attacked the other dogs and inevitably had to be put to sleep.

My question to you right now, is how will you go into combat? Will you use thus says the Lord or will you be saying to your enemy, I think I can? It's your choice.

Chapter 17

When God Feels Far Away

"Someday the sun is going to shine down on me in some faraway place." —MAHAILIA JACKSON

In my lifetime, I have asked why, and I was tired of asking. It was exhausting for me to try to reach God because He was so far away—from my reach. Like anyone else on this great big planet of ours, I was so tired of suffering. However, I understand now why I suffered in the first place and why I should not be surprised in the future. [1] It was not easy growing up and not having my questions answered. I wanted answers or a sign but didn't get them. When was this God going to show himself? I am sure that I have not been the only one who has felt this way. I'm sure you know what I mean. Why do bad things happen to good people? What is it about the good people that they must suffer more than the not so good?

Why members of the same household experience different circumstances for example one child could be happy and the other extremely miserable? I often thought that it wasn't fair. Then I came to Christ and reached an understanding that there is an answer to my WHY God?

Well, the unfortunate answer is very simple. We live in a sinful world with many individuals who have freedom of choice and a free will. (John 16:33) NKJV states, *"These things I have spoken to you, that in Me you may have peace. In the world you will have tribulations; but be of good cheer, I have overcome the world."*

Although I did not agree with the verse at first, I had a choice to rethink and agree or not. I was exercising my right to choose and although minimal as it may seem, everyone has a choice, whether big or small and make the right or wrong decisions in life. I chose to follow Satan with my eyes wide open and mind narrowly shut, but when I came to the Lord, I chose to follow Him with my mind, body and soul. Choosing Christ does not mean that I am automatically exempt from experiencing pain. Remember, I was not forced into the Lord's Army; I came in alone, because God sought me out in the depths of hell, and now, I desire to help others be loosened from Satan's tight grip.

This brings me to Job. Job was a true warrior for God. Do you know the story of Job? I chose Job for two reasons, one because of how much I loathed this story in my past and because how much I appreciate it now. For those who have not heard of Job and his life, come take a small journey into his life with me.

The Bible states, *"There was a man in the land of Uz, whose name was Job; and that man was blameless and upright, and one who feared God and shunned evil" "So it was when the days of feasting had run their course that He would send and sanctify them, and he would rise early in the morning and offer burnt offering according to the number of them all. For Job said 'It may be that my sons have sinned and cursed God in their hearts' Thus Job did this regularly"* (Job 1:5) NKJV

Wow, what a loving father to ask for forgiveness for his children. This was an awesome man of God; however, things did not stay so beautiful and wonderful as you read further. *"Now there was a day when the sons of God came to present themselves before the Lord, and Satan also came among them"* (Job 1:6) NKJV.

Yes! You read correctly, "and Satan also came among them." This points' out two things: Satan does exist and there were sons of God that went before God to present themselves. Now, why would Satan try to infiltrate? Why would Satan even approach God in the first place? The story plot thickens. In (Job 1:7), the Lord said to Satan, *"From where do you come?"* as if the Lord did not know. *Then Satan answered the Lord and said, "From going to and fro on the earth, and from walking back and forth on it"* (Job 1:8) NKJV. I strongly believe this is where a normal person would cringe, for I did and I got upset at God. *"Have you considered My servant Job, that there is none like him on the earth, a blameless and upright man, one who fears God and shuns evil?"* Hello! I always read this story as a child and questioned, *"God, how can you do this? How can you allow this to happen?"* So Satan answered the Lord and said, *"Does Job fear God for nothing?"* (Job 1:9) NKJV. WAIT A MINUTE!!! God was talking to Satan and making a wager?

Does He not clearly see what is going on? Why would God do this? In the next verse, Satan continues in this dialogue asking God, *"Have You not made a hedge around him, around his household and around all that he has on every side? You have blessed the work of his hands, and his possessions have increased in the land"* (Job 1:10) NKJV. *"But now, stretch your hand and touch all that he has and he will surely curse you to your face!"* (Job 1:11) NKJV. My interpretation of this verse tells me that Satan was tempting God. This was clearly a test. It is written! *"For we do not wrestle against flesh and blood, but against principalities, against powers against the rulers of the darkness of this age, against spiritual hosts of wickedness in the heavenly places?"* (Ephesians 6:12) NKJV. I would say this is evidence that these things do happen. This is absolutely "spiritual warfare" and God is in control at all times, even though it may not seem that way. But why would God do this? What was the point? Could it be that He used Job as an example for us today?

I truly believe that if we have faith, God will not give us more than we can handle; although hard to swallow, it is true. Only He knows the future. In (Romans 8:28) NKJV, the verse starts with, *"And we know"*—now, "and we know" this should be a confirmation from someone that really believes in God—*"And we know that all things work together for good to those who love God, to those who are the called according to His purpose."*

Do you hear me? Are you getting the story?

Let's read further. *"So the Lord said to Satan, 'behold, all that he has is in your power; only do not lay a hand on his person'"* (Job 1:12) NKJV. Then Satan went out from the presence of the Lord. What is most interesting in this verse is that the Lord gave Satan power. Satan could not do a thing to Job unless God granted Satan the power.

Can you see this meeting between God and Satan discussing Job? One by one, Satan hits Job with affliction, death, disease, betrayal, and loneliness, and still after all was said and done to him, you read that God not only reinstated Job but He also gave Job a new family, home and a new life.. *"Now the Lord blessed the latter days of Job more than this beginning; for he had fourteen thousand sheep, six thousand camels, one thousand yoke of oxen, and one thousand female donkeys"* (Job 1:13) NKJV. *"He also had seven sons and three daughters"* (Job 1:17) NKJV. *"So Job died, old and full of days"* (Job 42:12-13) NKJV. Did God use Job and others in the Bible for examples so that we would know we are not alone? I have often felt that way, but unlike Job, I have failed many tests in life.

Whether it is your uncle, father, brother, sister, mother, or friend that hurt you, there is no easy way to describe the pain you're suffering from. We must be careful not to allow our hearts to be filled with anger and resentment because the enemy will enter. It did not take much time before Satan settled in and set up camp in my heart, planting all types of seeds of lies, in my heart and mind. Satan will use everyone nearest and dearest to you. In Job's situation, he began with the only remaining member of his household, his wife.

Have you ever asked yourself why Job's wife didn't die? For the longest I thought the wife remained for the purpose of nagging or maybe to be used as a tool of Satan, but in time I learned that Job's wife remained because God knew her heart and He wished her to remain. She probably couldn't stand seeing her husband in pain, remember she too was hurting; she also experienced loss along with Job. Job knew who he was in God. Do you know who you are in Christ? Let us reflect. Earlier, we learned that prayer and knowledge of the Word will help identify our true enemy, and will empower us to triumph. We also learned that if we do not have the proper tools, the fight is already lost.

Job knew who he was in God, and he understood that God was his only hope. , "Do you know who you are?"

Chapter 18

Awaken the Silence: When Silence Isn't Golden

We are hard pressed on every side, but not crushed. Perplexed, but not in despair. Persecuted, but not abandoned. Struck down, but not destroyed— II CORINTHIANS 4: 8-9 NKJV

Is there sexual abuse in the churches today? I can honestly answer that question with a big YES! We must awaken the silence that is killing our young, spiritually and physically, in our churches. Let me tell you to what extreme Satan took me, because the silence was killing me. I tried to run from God, even to the point that I rebelled so much that I was practicing witchcraft and voodoo, vacillating back and forth from God to Satan. I began to tell myself that there was no God and no Satan. For those who do not believe that there is a Satan or even Lucifer, that is a lie. We know from reading the story of Job that Satan does exist and he used to speak with God. Knowing that there was a Satan, and although I forgave my past abusers—I could not surrender to God completely. It should not surprise you that Satan has had thousands of years to experiment with many lies. One can find the first lie that Satan used on humankind when he spoke with Eve. It should also not surprise you when I tell you that I began to believe that maybe, "I am a child of Satan."

As you may recall, Edward the rapist and Marty the molester, were both deacons in the church when I was a child, in fact, my sources say that they still hold some sort of position in the church and easy access to children and although I have been responsible to mention this to the higher powers, they still remain in their positions. That frustrates me to no end but I must press on.

For many of us survivors, we have carried this burden and self-hatred in our lives. It is time to let go of our burdens and give them to Jesus.[1] There were three times that I attempted suicide because of the burdens that I carried. It was only by the grace of God, did He allow me to live. I have a question for you, how long have you been carrying your burden? How many of us have suffered at the hands of an abuser, molester, or rapist? How many nightmares are you having—the demons that reminds us of our past and the ridicules of others? The church must heal, but this cannot happen until we awaken the silence.

Have you become a prisoner in your mind, unable to cope with the present? For some, our pain is as fresh as the day it began. Some of us were born into a family of pain and secrets, limiting our chances of recovery.

Who am I and why am I here? What is my purpose in this life? You long to be normal, but you do not know what it is to be normal. You hunger, but you do not know what you need to fill the emptiness in your gut and in your spirit? You thirst like Christ on the cross but those around you give you vinegar.

The constant reminder of where you have been, not where you are, continues to bombard your thoughts. You close your eyes and your constant thoughts now manifest in to mini little movie trailers, racing through your mind. Your dreams have no hope and your vision is dimmed. To trust is to die, like being naked in a crowd. You are slowly dying, but you do not want to die. You hang on for dear life only to be disappointed. I know; I have been there.

Only you, by the grace of God, can stop the cycle and awaken the silence. How can you stop the cycle? Seek a Christian counselor that specializes in childhood abuses, start or attend a recovery group and once you heal, use your testimony to help others. In my case, what I have learned is that God gave me gifts and wanted me to use them for His purpose. Satan tried to quiet me down, but I am speaking. Although, I had other agendas, God saw a way for me to speak up and help others who are hurting from their past or their lives now. In truth, during my vacillation period, I asked for "the great time of persecution among Christians" to begin, so that I could destroy them. It is no big secret that Satan is trying to destroy our churches by using former Christians that were once hurt and have not recovered.

What treasures do you have to offer the good Lord? When God calls, He gives you many ways to answer. If we do not answer the call He will send another form of communication that we can understand. Sometimes we want to use our treasures, but we just do not know how because we are told not to or that we are not good enough, but if you love to sing, sing for the Lord, if you love to write, write for the Lord, whatever it is that you love, use your treasures for the Lord. Whatever it is that you have wanted to do for God, you can start right now do it for God. Everyone must use his or her gifts to awaken the silence. Anyone who knows me will tell you that I am a modern-day Jonah. The story of Jonah is not my favorite story at all. As you have read, for many years the Lord had called me, however, because of vacillating spirit I could not see what the true God wanted me to do for Him. I would ask myself, who is this God to think I can do anything for Him?

Why me? Well, why not me? In the spring of 2005, after many challenges and surrendering my tiny million-dollar business, God confirmed to me what I was trying to avoid. Since then, I have been working with the Lord to teach members of churches to awaken the silence. Deadly silence is spreading throughout all denominations, the world is now in the churches and we must put an end to it. We cannot point fingers at one specific church. Sexual, physical, emotional, power and mental abuse is not only in the world, but it is destroying lives, families and individuals in our very own congregations. Be knowledgeable and protect our children from sexual predators. If you're interested in knowing more about protecting the children, a child Molestation Prevention Plan can be found in the back of the book.

Chapter 19

God Cannot Do...

"God creates, God is a God of miracles, God is a sovereign God, God calls life into existence, and God places His hands on the hurting heart, but... God cannot go against His word and this is the God that I serve." —VIVIONNE "GRACE" KELI

Everything that is happening on Earth today, including alarming increases of cannibalism, human trafficking, witchcraft, alternative lifestyles, war, child pornography, domestic violence, crimes of all sorts, and so on will be blamed on God by someone somewhere. In all honesty, I too, have been guilty, at one time or another, of blaming Him. As you have read in previous chapters, in 2004, I had the opportunity to be reintroduced to God after vacillating back and forth. This time, I got to know God for myself—a loving and caring God. I began to understand His beauty.

How well do you know the God of Abraham, Isaac, and Jacob, the God of Israel? Do you know what He is capable of doing? Do you know that we must be like Him in character? It is one thing to know someone and another is to try to be that someone. It is impossible to be someone that you are not, but it is possible to know them so well that you feel that you can be like them. For so many years, I loathed the God I had learned of when I was a child. I never desired to be like Him at all.

Even though it was instilled as children that our main objective was to become like Christ in character, I could not understand how to accomplish this. It was after my conversion that I understood how. It was by understanding what God cannot do. In order to get to know who God is, you must know what He can and cannot do. It is a blessing and a joy to know that God cannot do everything. You read it correctly. God cannot do everything, although capable, for He is God, He still cannot do everything.

I will elaborate more in depth as you read along. I know that once or twice in our lifetime, we have thought that God was not taking care of us the way we would have like or desired, but He did. You may be surprised that even the strongest Bible scholars and prayer warriors have experienced this dilemma of questioning God. Let's take a good look to see what He has done, is doing and will do. What He has done can be found in Genesis, when He created the heavens and the earth, the light and darkness, and all living creatures to inhabit the earth. [1]

The story of creation confirms what God can do. He created man and woman to live peacefully and in unity on Earth, with free choice to do whatever they pleased. They were in charge of the Earth. God was not only the Author of creation, but also the Creator, presenting husband and wife to the Universe.

In all His works, He did well. His only request to man and woman is found in (Genesis 2:16-17) NKJV *"And the Lord God commanded the man, saying, of every tree of the garden you may freely eat; (17) but of the tree of the knowledge of good and evil you shall not eat, for in the day that you eat of it you shall surely die."* Why would God allow this to happen? If He is all-knowing, would He then not know of what we, as humans, were capable of doing? But He is God and he knew what we would do but He gave us a choice and we chose incorrectly.

Now for my earlier statement that God cannot do everything. I thank God for the things that He cannot do. I am thankful that God cannot and will not hate me for the color of my skin for I am His daughter. He cannot treat me like garbage for He created me in His image and knew me before I was even conceived. I am thankful that He cannot make us into robots without free choice.

God won't make us do anything we do not want to do. Do not get me wrong, God has been known to seek the lost, for He is the Good Shepherd. [2] He allows us to place ourselves in different situations, and has been known to place a road block or two in our paths to lead us back home, but He won't make you do anything you do not choose to do.

As history tells us, He even sent a fish to swallow Jonah, so that he would do God's will. But God cannot make you change your mind. He is persistent and rightfully so. Hitler knew of God, but he chose to be evil, destroying millions of lives in concentration camps. That was his choice. I will admit when God wants someone, He will do His will to get His lost sheep, but inevitably, only you have the choice to say, "Yes Lord, I am your servant" or say, "Forget it I do not want any part of it." God is a God of choices; you either love Him or hate Him, it is either one or the other.

The murderer has a choice to walk away or to kill. Let me stop here for a moment, it would be irresponsible and ignorant of me to disregard the fact that some people, committing heinous crimes may have imbalances in their chemical structure or may be possessed by demonic forces, but they too have a choice. Society has found ways to blame parents, environments, and DNA, which can be legitimate arguments to one's demise in life, but to include God in the blame game is also a choice and a terrible one at that. The blame game has been mastered since Adam first blamed Eve for the fall of humankind.[3] Were you aware that blaming others involves mentally removing oneself, negating responsibilities and accountabilities? This process of thinking is, in fact, a choice. No matter how you slice it, you have a choice. God cannot go against His commandments. He cannot lie and because of this, I can rest on His promises, especially when He says, *"I will never leave you nor forsake you"* (Hebrew 13:5) NKJV. Even though my life may be falling apart, I know that He will not leave me and definitely not forsake me.

God will not go against His own word. I have heard, at times and more recently, of couples complaining that their spouses are bad for them, but that God placed a special person in their lives that they consider a blessing. Soon, they are romantically involved with the "special person," complicating their situation. Hello! If you are married and have a "special person" in your life, other than your spouse and you're romantically involved, you are committing ADULTERY. God did not put this person in your life for you to fall. I mean, seriously, think about it. If adultery was not important, God would not have placed it in His law, *"You shall not commit adultery"* (Exodus 20:14) NKJV.

No matter how good the person may seem, God cannot accept your adulterous behavior, so do not expect God to bend the rules for you. God cannot go against the fiber of His being and His very existence because it is not in His nature. Remember, God cannot lead you to sin. If both couples are married and one spouse desires the other man's wife or the other women's husband; that is called COVETOUSNESS. It does not matter how bad the situation is in your marriage God cannot give you someone else's spouse because you are hurting while you have your own spouse. *"You shall not covet your neighbor's house; you shall not covet your neighbor's wife, nor his manservant, nor his maidservant, nor his ox nor his donkey, nor anything that is your neighbor's"* (Exodus 20:17) NKJV.

If you are not married and having sex, it is never too late to become pure again in the sight of God, according to (1John 1:7) NKJV, *"But if we walk in the light as He is in the light, we have fel-*

lowship with one another, and the blood of Jesus Christ His Son cleanses us from all sins." Nevertheless, if you continue in your sin, that is called FORNICATION. It is written, *"Marriage is honorable among all, and the bed undefiled but fornicators and adulterers God will judge"* (Hebrew 13:4) NKJV.

If you have children out of wedlock and have not married in the eyes of God, and are having sex outside of marriage, called "common law," it is FORNICATION. What kind of God would God be if He allowed you to continue to sin? I know firsthand, because before my conversion I was guilty of this as well.

Several years ago, I was asked to speak on my experiences in the occult and the practice of voodoo, I agreed. My sermon, "The Christian Witch," covered many issues that are invading churches and Christian colleges today. Many parents do not understand that there are lots of things that do not edify God, which by default, automatically edifies Satan. In churches, I have seen youth with relics, signs, and dress codes that clearly are leading our youth into Satan's very hands. When I thought that I had the power to call upon the dead, be a medium, read tarot cards, perform incantations and spells, I was inviting demons to take possession of me. People don't understand that the things they buy, hear, see and even expose themselves to, if they are not of God, they are inviting the demonic forces into their lives. We need to be covered with the blood of Jesus Christ at all times so these demons cannot invade our territory. It is not my mission to be a sensationalist; it is my duty, to inform Christians that witchcraft exists in some form or another in different denominations. I praise God that I have been clean and sober from the intoxication of witchery since March 2004. As with any vice, I must keep my mind clear and not expose myself to demonic movies, videos, questionable music, or even some locations. Actually, I abstain from anything that could and will alter my senses, rule of thumb, if it does not glorify God,

I will not partake of it. The simplest of things are the ones that can place you in Satan's grips.

Even your smallest trinkets that represent lucky charms, you are exposing your mind to things of the occult. Paying for things that are of the occult, no matter how you look at it,—even if you do not consider yourself a practicing witch—you are contributing to the occult. Whether you want to admit it or not, you are practicing by supporting WITCHCRAFT. *"There shall not be found among you anyone who makes his son or his daughter pass through the fire, or one who practices witchcraft, or a soothsayer, or one who interprets omens, or a sorcerer, or one who conjures spells or a medium, or a spiritist, or one who calls up the dead. For all who do these things are an abomination to the Lord, and because of these abominations the Lord your God drives them out from before you"* (Deuteronomy 18:10 -12) NKJV.

If you like to role-play that you are sleeping with a child sexually, keep questionable pictures of children on your computer, or you or someone you know fantasizes about having a relationship with a child, then you or they are traveling the path of a MOLESTER/PEDOPHILE. This is your opportunity to surrender to God and **seek professional help!!!**

Throughout my years, I have counseled as a friend and a survivor on several topics using my testimony and I have heard the many legitimate reasons people leave their marriages. They try to tell me as to why they cannot forgive a person that has caused them great pain; or why people hate their parents. Why would you think that God will understand your reasoning as to why you killed or hate your enemy? Think about this, if they did it to Jesus Christ, why not you?

My friend, these are lies created by Satan. By thinking that God will allow you to take vengeance into your own hands is ruling out God's word. Thus says the Lord God, *"Beloved, do not avenge yourselves, but rather give place to wrath; for it is written, 'Ven-*

geance is Mine, I will repay.' Therefore if your enemy hungers, feed him; If he thirsts, give him a drink; for in so doing you will heap coals of fire on his head" (Romans 12:19-20) NKJV.

You may say to yourself, *"Oh but, you do not understand how I feel. I want to make my spouse pay for all the hurt she/he has caused me and this is the very reason that I believe that God placed this person in my life—so I can see what I am missing or be loved."* WRONG. In no way will God go against His teaching. Listen my friend, I can tell you that I know about this topic personally, because I also had my legitimate excuses. As you recall in one of my chapters, I was in my late twenties when I reached a spiritual fork in the road. Walter and I would have domestic fights; they would get worse and worse as the years progressed. My future did not seem at all promising, and then I met Steven. He was God sent, and I was in love. I thought, God knows my past and my pains and this was the answer. It all started with Bible lessons and prayer, but one thing led to another and when we realized it, we were consumed in lust, not love. Did God place Steven in my life to bring me joy? "No!"

We often attempt to "help" God because He is taking too long. When Sarah was told she was to bear a child in her old age, did she have faith when she gave Hagar to Abraham to bear an offspring? No! Doesn't God want what is best for us? [4] God cannot make us do anything we do not want or desire to do. Because of this, if we don't have a relationship with God, more often than not, it will be through our free choice that we will continue to make our mistakes.

Now that you know what God cannot do, we can focus on what He can and will do. You must have FAITH and trust that God desires the best for you.

In Sarah's case, she lacked faith because she was old and could not envision the possibility of giving birth to a child. But, look what God did. He still provided Sarah with Isaac. Are we reaping the consequences of Sarah's mistrust of God? Yes! Look at the war we are having today in Iraq. This is Ishmael's seed always fighting with Isaac's seed. Getting to know God's word and His voice must be our daily focus. Relying and depending on Him should be your quest in life! Thus says the Lord in Matthew 6:28-33:

> So why do you worry about clothing? Consider the lilies of the field, how they grow: they neither toil nor spin; (29) and yet I say to you that even Solomon in all his glory was not arrayed like on of these. (30) Now if God so clothes the grass of the field, which today is and tomorrow is thrown into the oven, will He not much more clothe you, **O you of little faith?** (31) Therefore do not worry, saying, what shall we eat? Or what shall we drink?' or what shall we wear? (32) For after all these things the Gentiles seek. For your heavenly Father knows that you need all these things. (33) But seek first the kingdom of God and His righteousness, and all these things shall be added to you.

Oh, you of little faith, that is the whole focus of this chapter; building faith in a God that cannot go contrary to His word. That is, if you hold fast and hold on to every letter of His word, He will give you all the desires of your heart, according to His will. How do you get to know this awesome God? It is easy. How do you work on healthy relationships on Earth? Constant communication through phone calls, emails, and correspondence allows you to build your relationships. This also applies to God, but God must take precedence over everything you do—even more than our strongest relationship on Earth. Whatever it is, a good spouse, mate, home, car, or finances—that you are in need of, you must have faith and know what your God can do. When was the last time you opened your Bible? When was the last time you called Him up and told Him what you want? Getting to know God must be your ever pressing focus and depending on Him must be engraved in your heart, mind, and soul, each day you get up and before you sleep, as well as in your travels and business.

The core of your being should emanate the presence of God through your actions, words, and appearance. Once you get to know God, you will desire to be like Him. I ask you right now, to take inventory and assess your walk with God. How well do you know Him? What is He capable of doing and not doing? What can He do and what can He not do? Remember, what's most important is simply being true to God! God cannot lead you to a sinful life; only YOU can choose. Whom will you choose today? Give your burdens, your pain, your hurts, your past, your now, and your future to God.

Chapter 20

Surrendering to Forgiveness

"When we know love matters more than anything, and we know that nothing else REALLY matters, we move into the state of surrender. Surrender does not diminish our power, it enhances it." —SARA PADDISON

Did you know that you are more than a conqueror! "Yet in all these things we are more than conquerors through Him who loved us" (Romans 8:37) NKJV. As warriors and survivors, we have conquered more than most, but it is not just about merely surviving; it is about a new way of living. Surrendering to forgiveness is a way of life, a vital way of living. For some reason, in my darkest hours, I often thought of Jana Thurber and Pastor Mic. Jana was married to Pastor "Mic." This couple really loved their youth and the youth knew it, for I was one of them. Jana tried to figure out what was going on in my life, but I could not tell her about the abuse at that time. I did not trust anyone out side of the family. When I became a young mother, I attempted to go back to church for a moment; Jana came and gave me Bible lessons. Unfortunately, we only met a few times because Walter did not want anyone over the house. However, Jana left me thinking about who I was, in Christ, and although she planted a seed in me, I couldn't imagine any remedy for the pain I was enduring with Walter.

What I learned from Jana resonated in my spirit. Until one day, it hit me and I understood what Jana told me many years earlier. The Lord brought her counsel to the forefront of my mind and I was able to understand that the seed of forgiveness would one day be my calling.

You see, what Jana told me about Jesus' ministry was really based on love, forgiveness, and peace among many other ministries that He had. *"Forbearing one another, and forgiving one another, if any man has a quarrel against any; even as Christ forgave you, so also do ye" (Colossians 3:13) NKJV.* A message to our youth and young adult leaders, plant the seed, that is your responsibility, and God will do His work sooner or later. Do not give up on the youth and although you may not see the seed flourish don't give up. Jana's talk seemed to have fallen on deaf ears but they somehow managed to remain in my heart during all of my hell days. Don't give up on the youth, love them and show them God's love.

God placed the Thurber's, Bruni, Rachel, Pastor Carl Rodriguez, Dorothy Macey and others in my path until I made that choice. I am glad that God is persistent. Has God placed someone in your life that attempted to encourage you to seek Him through scripture like that of Jana and Pastor Mic Thurber and the rest of His warriors? Start today, the Savior is calling you. [1] He is strategically placing people around you that are Christ focused so that you come under His banner of love. Why? Because He loves you! [2] You better believe that someone is planting a seed for your good... Become a fruitful bearer, blossom in our Lord Jesus Christ and see the transformation that only He can give.

If you have been a victim by a so-called Christian, let me take this opportunity to say to you "I'm so sorry." You see, Christians are not all perfect and although that is not an excuse, find it in your heart to forgive and let go. Let God deal with these individuals but don't give up on God. Release them and come home.

You see, forgiveness does not mean letting people get away with murder, but it does mean that you do not have to spend any more energy on those who violated you. Forgive yourself, embrace yourself, become a friend to yourself. Give God another chance. Even though you may have felt He was not there for you, He was. You may not know why things happened, but God has always been there for you.

Without forgiveness, I would not be here today, living a powerful and dynamic life. I had the great opportunity to sit on the board of a ministry called, *End* Times like These Ministries for a short while. We assist communities with recovery, restoration, and retention programs; focusing on every aspect of a person's life. The program is entitled, Serve-To-Save.

The thought of meeting individuals who have gone through far worse than me and having the opportunity to help them in their recovery and restoration phase is incredible and magnificent.

I have re-entered my daughters' lives. My relationship with my family is great because I learned to set boundaries. My stepmother Nelda and I are best of friends. I love my former husband and his wife, and although I have forgiven them, sometimes, they tend to make me forget, but it gets better and better each day. I pray for their salvation and I pray for my past abusers that one day they will be ready for the day of reckoning. I have a great husband and I'm able to help others who have traveled the same path. I am still work in progress, however, without recovery; I would not have been able to resume getting my education. In the spring of 2010, and with God's grace, I will be entering the Psy.D. program. I choose to live a life of abundance and no matter what comes my way; I know that I make the choice to be happy or sad. It is what you make of life not what life makes of you.

Choosing how you think and how you perceive your situation will more often than not, dictate your life. With this said, had I not changed my perspectives in life, I would still be living in the past, wondering if God had sent His wrath on my enemies. What a waste of precious time that will never be regained. No rollover minutes…What a shame!

What if I told you that you are alive today because God has allowed you to live another day; would you believe me? Don't you know that if you have endured childhood traumas and adult suffering that you are a survivor? You have beaten statistics? Most adults who have endured childhood abuses end up, on drugs, on the streets, dying of AIDS, in jail, in mental hospitals, homeless, generational victims, having babies from different partners or in some cases, are dead. Except for the dead, all that have been mentioned in the above statement also have a choice to become pure or remain in their muck. That is the beauty of our Lord and Savior Jesus Christ, come as you are and He will transform you into what you were meant to be.

I know that if you are reading this book, you are an excellent candidate to ask God into your life and begin to heal this very moment.

What I would suggest for you is to make a list of everyone you must forgive. Granted, there may be some individuals that you may never get the opportunity to speak to in person, but that should not stop you from placing them on your list, praying for them, and understanding that God is in control and will deal with these people accordingly. Forgive your past mistakes. We blame ourselves for things we had no control over or of which we were ignorant of. A small child is certainly not responsible for the abuse committed against him or her. As I have mentioned several times in my previous chapters, look for a counselor that specializes in helping survivors. Join a group of survivors or start a group at your church. Find someone to mentor you during these times.

Forgiveness will also help you by giving you a new perspective on life. It will help you understand that you and I have freedom to choose life, and that the individuals who robbed us of our innocence, dignity, and self-worth exercised their free choice. Do not blame yourself for what someone else did to you and don't blame someone else for what mistakes you choose for yourself. God has given us the Bible, a manual for living. Know God's law and use the armor He has supplied you with. You are a warrior now; you have been called.

Begin a new relationship with God. Read His Word. God loves you, no matter what the world says. Pray and search Him diligently. Again, I stress, give God another chance, believe it or not, people get appalled when I say this.

God knows everything about you and God does not care where you have been but rather He desires that you are in Him. It is through Christ that we are made whole. [3] It is written *"Therefore, if anyone is in Christ, he is a new creation; old things have passed away; behold, all things have become new"* (2 Corinthians 5:17) NKJV What I've gone through, in the past, has caused me to make some wrong decisions, but I have become new in Christ.

It was July 19, 2005, when I began to see where God was leading me. I had finished studying scriptures when I realized what true conversion was all about. True conversion, my friends, is allowing God to change you from what you once were. When I came back to God I knew that only He could change my life and thought processes. I had a new identity—a "Re-Born Identity" that cannot be faked or manipulated. Christ became my example and slowly, I began to change, but not by my own doing. How did I know that I was changing? I didn't! That was the beauty of it...I had no clue that I was changing. The change was seen by others but not necessarily by me. The few things I did notice about myself were, I was able to control my temper much better than I had in the past, and I was able to forgive, others for their wrong doing toward me and not waste time seeking revenge.

I believe that if a person gives themselves to Christ, that in time, they will have a Re-born identity as well. However, so often, new believers take on the identity of other Christians instead of Christ and then they are back where they started…empty. It was my desire that when I came back to God that I would not allow myself to conform to the behaviors of others. It was important to remember what I liked and disliked about the Christians that I grew up with and not become like them. In fact, I used to say that I was raised by Bulimic and Cannibal Christians.

What is a bulimic Christian? These Christians purchased all the right books, heard all the right sermons, purchased all the latest Christian movies, attended every Christian event they could possibly attend, and took in massive Christian information; to only spit it out when they got fed up. The WORD of the Lord was not rooted, in their bodies long enough, to keep them nourished. They became slim in the word and eventually died of spiritual starvation. These individuals were unbalanced and spiritually malnourished. I was raised with bulimic Christians and eventually, most of these Christians left the church wanting nothing to do with God. They, as we all are, still struggling with their spiritual walk. They look good on the outside but inside they are dead.

What is a Cannibal Christian? These Christians watch everything they do; they believe in image and remind me of a modern day Pharisee. These Christians make sure they live piously. They keep themselves from any "secular" activities including wearing pants, wearing make-up, wearing jewelry, watching television, hearing the radio unless the station is from their own faith, they don't drink coffee or eat pork (good thing), abstain from having fun with others, and are judgmental of others who are not of the same faith, class or don't possess the level of education that meets their approval. They pay their tithe (a good thing), and believe in taking care of their bodies by being vegetarians or vegan (excellent thing).

These Christians try to have everything in place and most often become very pious and anyone that goes against their faith or thought process is an infidel.

The Cannibal Christian has mastered spiritual cannibalism. They may be strict vegetarians or even vegan; but spiritually they will devour anyone in the name of God. They seem to always be right, because they read all the right books, wear the right clothes and know the right people. I was raised predominately with these types of Christians. They had the right message, but they did not live the message of redemption.

These are the Christians that worry me the most, because they seem all together however, they are not aware that their tongue is killing others spiritually. They did not understand that their actions and their words did hurt people. I used to say to myself about them that, "Sticks and stones can break the bones but word will always harm me." When I came back, I vowed to the Lord that I wouldn't be like either of these types of Christian.

How do we keep from becoming either? The answer my friends, is through constant prayer and following the example given to us in the Bible. Jesus is the only perfect example. I am aware that we will never be exactly like Christ however; all He asks of us is that we strive in Him. If we were perfect, we would all be in heaven and I wouldn't be writing a book about forgiveness.

Only you can choose what kind of Christian you want to be. What matters is your personal relationship with God. When one is truly converted they take on a Re-Born identity.

I still come across bulimic and cannibal Christians and let me tell you, that when I go and give my testimonial, some come and tell me that they cannot believe what I have gone through.

Actually, some of these believers tell me that I should maybe change my testimony so that I do not scare others away but, the truth is truth.

I have gone through hell and have been a hostess to demons, but, that is the past and Christ reigns in my heart now. Other believers do not always know how to interact with me. A few are scared of me, and are convinced I am still practicing witchcraft. And on many occasions I have simply been called a liar to my face, because to them my story is unfathomable…why are Christians so afraid of what's real? The bottom line is not what they believe, but what God knows about me. In fact, a female pastor gave me a book regarding coming out of spiritual darkness which was given to her by a church member, to give to me, anonymously, after I told my testimony.

People do not understand that anonymously rebuking someone is worse than, out of love, coming to his or her brother in Christ and talking with them. Funny I thought, little did they know, I already had the book, and was encouraging others who were spiritually afflicted and in darkness to read the same book. When I received it, I did not get angry, I actually prayed for both the person that was judging me and the pastor for being a tool. This pastor did not know that she was being used by Satan to tear me down, she thought it was out of love.

All I can do for those that do not receive my testimony is to pray for them, and still press on because I know where God has rescued me from. Some believers do not understand that they are being used by Satan; trying to be better than others because they do not understand the true meaning of surrender, conversion and transformation.

Christ has a message for these so-called "believers" that I love to quote. This very message is for those *"believers"* who think they are the chosen ones.

"Not everyone who says to Me, 'Lord, Lord,' shall enter the kingdom of heaven, but he who does the will of My Father in heaven. Many will say to Me in that day, 'Lord, Lord, have we not prophesied in Your name, cast out demons in Your name, and done many wonders in Your name?' (Matthew 7: 21, 22) NKJV

Now, for those who desire to come back home to Christ, remember, the world and some "so-called believers" will reject God's word but the ultimate rejection in my eyes is when God claims you as His son or daughter or rejects you for eternity.

As for me, when "believers" question my testimony, I must remember, I am doing my Father's will by telling others my testimony and how God rescued me from above. Getting rejected by others is nothing in comparison to being rejected by my Father in Heaven. Jesus will one day say to some of us:

"I never knew you; depart from Me, you who practice lawlessness!" (Matthew7:23) NKJV

God is always in control. He's not here to scare you. But we are not really in control of our lives as the world makes us believe. Each day, we are given yet another chance to make a difference and to seek God. If you have suffered and felt that God is not worth giving another chance to, let me beseech you my sisters and brothers to rethink. Do not miss the opportunity of a lifetime to know God for Who He is.

For so many years, I was depressed because I allowed my past to control my circumstances, not allowing God to do what He does best, which is recovery of the mind, body and soul. I avoided reading the Word and following God because there were too many rules. Do you wonder why God has rules? Because God knows our hearts and He knows us better than we know ourselves. When I chose to walk away from God, He allowed me to go through the process. Out of love, I am asking you today, have you asked God in your life? Have you really released your past mistakes and learned from them?

Let me recap, God placed many in my path but I still chose the path most frequented. What area of your life do you think God has been working in? Start listening to those around you and see who has God placed in your life. They are in your life because God is calling you back home.

We have touched on many subjects, in this book, and as this final chapter ends, I pray that you see that without forgiveness, prayer, surrender and knowing what camp you are in, you become an easy target for Satan. Not having knowledge of the law or God, and not being prepared for the enemies attack, you too, will fall into Satan's trap every time.

We must be grounded in the Word but unfortunately, too often, we are misguided by traditions, unloving believers, past experiences, and failed theories. These things hinder us from becoming effective warriors. We need God. When I say give God a chance, I mean get to know God—that is, the living God—not by what you were taught as a child that has not worked before, or traditions or because your family went to a certain church, but rather get to know Him as the adult that you are now. The time for change is now; learn to be good fruit for others, and learn to choose good fruit for you.

"A good tree cannot bear bad fruit, nor *can* a bad tree bear good fruit. Every tree that does not bear good fruit is cut down and thrown into the fire. Therefore *"by their fruits you will know them."* (Matthew 7:19, 20) NKJV

Once you allow God to heal you, you will be able to use your testimony to help others. You will bear good fruits once you surrender all to Jesus and follow the simple God inspired Word—the Bible.

Where ever you are, God is chastening you to come home to Him. I am so thankful that He chastened me when I was doing wrong. I know that God loves me; know that he loves you too.

The verse that is most fitting for me, as I close this chapter, is about the reason why the Lord gives us the Law and rebukes us when we do wrong—because He loves us. The word says in (Hebrews12:5, 6) *"My son, do not despise the chastening of the Lord, Nor be discouraged when you are rebuked by Him; for whom the Lord loves He chastens, and scourges every son whom He receives."*

We are survivors and warriors because there is a battle of good and evil, the question is whom are you fighting for and at what cost? We must know that if we are not being attacked by Satan then there is a problem. We do not have to look for problems; they will come.

My story in comparison to the rest of humanity is nothing but a brief story among a sea of stories. The wrong decisions and lack of faith in God cost me happiness during the first part of my life. I have not arrived yet, but I am a work in progress. I've reached a point in my Christian life where Heaven means more to me than anything this world has to offer. In fact, if you ask any of my friends I always say, I'd rather have someone **"rebuke me into heaven than love me right into hell."**

If you are trying to heal, once again, let me reiterate, find a Christian psychologist that deals with abuse cases. Join or start a group so that you can be the warrior for others. Ask your pastor, church leader, women's ministry leader, or personal ministries leader to begin classes and studies on domestic violence, sexual abuse and childhood traumas.

It is my prayer that your healing begins with you now. Give your mind, body and soul to Christ. Hold on to promises like (Isaiah 26:3) NKJV, *"You will keep him in perfect peace, whose mind is stayed on You, because he trusts in You."*

Also get planted and build yourself up in the Bible as you journey through "Root 66." Last but not least, because I love you and I know the pain that comes with abuse, I write the book. When I say that I enjoy life, I mean it. There are times when life seems unbearable, but knowing that I have a loving Father, makes it much easier to handle. Seek Him today and let Him use you for His good. Receive His peace today. And please know that you are not alone. Write to me and let me know who you are and how God has worked in your life? May God pour His blessings upon you as you embark on the journey to recovery.

ENDNOTES

All Bible passages are taken from the KJV

Chapter 1
[1] read John 10:10
[2] read 1 Corinthians 13:4-8
[3] read Proverbs 1:5
[4] read John 3:16
[5] read Exodus 14:14

Chapter 4
[1] read Genesis 5

Chapter 10
[1] Maritza Martin Munoz- was a victim of domestic violence who was murdered in cold blood by her former husband on Spanish television

Chapter 14
[1] read Psalm 119:105

Chapter 15
[1] read Romans 3:23
[2] read Philippians 2:5-7
[3] read Exodus 23:25

Chapter 17
[1] read John 16:33

Chapter 18
[1] read 1 Peter 5:7

Chapter 19
[1] read Genesis 1-3
[2] read John 10:11

[3] read Genesis 3:12
[4] read Jeremiah 29:11

Chapter 20
[1] read Revelation 3:20
[2] read John 3:16
[3] read Colossians 2:9-10

The Child Molestation Prevention Plan

Used By Permission

A Fact

Today, at least two out of every ten little girls and at least one out of every ten little boys are victims of a sexual abuser. That can change. We now have the power to stop the abusers who commit 95 percent of the sex acts against our children. We know who this abuser is, where to find him (or her), which children are most at risk, and how to protect them.

Your Opportunity To Save Children

"The Child Molestation Prevention Plan" explains the basic facts about child sexual abuse and presents a plan to protect children from molestation. In it you will learn:

- the definitions of child molester and child molestation;
- the damage caused by child sexual abuse;
- the characteristics of a child molester;
- the four general causes of child sexual abuse and the one cause responsible for 95 percent of all acts;
- how to identify and treat the single greatest cause early - before there is a victim;
- why The Child Molestation Prevention Plan will work.

1. Tell Others The Facts

What are the first three facts you can tell others? Fact one: Today, 95 percent of child molestation can be prevented. We have the knowledge to stop it. Fact two: Today, living in the United States, there are 39 million adults who have survived child sexual abuse. Fact three: Today, more than three million American children are victims. Most of them are children, struggling alone, believing there is no adult who can help them. To help prevent child molestation from happening to the children closest to you, begin by telling others the basic facts.

But why you? Shouldn't stopping sexual abuse be left to professionals - physicians and therapists? Better yet, shouldn't the police and the courts take care of it?

Professionals - physicians and therapists - can *never* put an end to sexual abuse; neither can the police or the courts. Why? Because they come on the scene too late. By the time they get there, the children have already been molested. Only you can get there in time.

There's a bigger reason why the professionals and the courts can't put an end to sexual abuse. They have no permission to talk to a child about sex - unless, of course, they talk to the child after the fact, after the child has already been sexually abused or has abused another child. Only *you* can talk to your children before anything happens, before any damage is done - to anyone.

Not In My Family

What if you are certain there has never been a child molester or a molested child in your family? You are probably wrong.

Unfortunately, most of today's children will never tell. They feel ashamed that this has happened to them. They are protecting their abuser because he or she is part of their family. They are protecting other members of their family - saving them from the pain of knowing.

In spite of the millions of victims in our families, many people stick to their mistaken belief that child molestation has nothing to do with them.

An estimated one in 20 teenage boys and adult men sexually abuse children, and an estimated one teenage girl or adult woman in every 3,300 females molests children. Although that's well over five million people, most families mistakenly believe that as far as molesters go, there has never been one in their family, and what's more, there never will be. Add together the child victims, the adult survivors, and the abusers, and that's 15 out of every 100 Americans who have been either a molested child or a molester.

To help prevent child molestation from happening to the children closest to you, begin by telling others the basic facts.

We Start By Speaking The Same Language

If we're going to work together to stop child sexual abuse, we have to speak the same language. We have to mean the same thing when we say "child molester," "child molestation," and even "child."

Moreover, all of us have to understand the basic facts: What exactly is child molestation? How many of our children are sexually abused? How seriously are they damaged? What are the characteristics of a child molester? What causes someone to sexually abuse a child? Which of our children are most at risk?

A **child molester** is any older child or adult who touches a child for his or her own sexual gratification.

Child molestation is the act of sexually touching a child.

A **child** is a girl or boy who is 13 years of age or younger.

What's the **age difference** between a molester and a child? It is five years, so a 14-year-old "older child" sexually touching a nine-year-old is an example. This is the accepted medical definition.

Sometimes, a professional will consider that a molestation act has occurred when the older child is only three years older - a sixth-grader with a third-grader, for instance. The crucial element here is the lack of equality between the two children; the sixth grader is clearly bigger, more powerful, and more "adult-like" than the third-grader.

We avoid definitions that are ambiguous by sticking to the medical definition. *We define "child molester" as an adult or child, who is at least five years older than the child he or she has molested.*

Telling Others The Facts

If we're going to protect our children from sexual abuse, all of us have to understand exactly what we mean by the act of sexual abuse. Why? Because one of the greatest obstacles we face is people's fear of the facts about child molestation.

For instance, some people who have no idea that sexual touch is vastly different from hugging are afraid to hug a child - especially one who isn't theirs - because someone might think they are child molesters. You can calm their fears by telling them this fact: Hugging is *not* molesting. Sexual touch is when an adult fondles the child's chest, buttocks, or genitals with the direct purpose of sexually exciting himself or the child.

Can you tell your husband that fact? Can you tell your sister, your cousin, or your best friend? If you can, then you can easily tell others all the rest of the facts.

The less people know, the more anxiety they feel, and the more they want to run away or pretend that today's estimated three million sexually abused children don't exist. Every fact has a calming effect. By telling the people closest to you the facts, you can help those same people become strong adult protectors of the children closest to you.

How Many Children Are Sexually Abused?

Three million children! I don't believe it. How can you possibly know that there are *exactly* three million child victims?" As you begin to tell others the facts, this is the first question they may ask you. The answer: Of course, we don't know *exactly*.

Children seldom tell. Those millions of children are a secret. They are the secret in family after family after family. Even adult survivors of childhood sexual abuse seldom tell. What we do know from studies of adult men and women is that the number is *at least* three million. At least three million children are molested before they finish their 13th year. In 1998, there were 103,000 reported *and confirmed* cases of child molestation. For comparison, at the height of the polio epidemic that struck children in the 1950s, there were 21,000 cases reported in a year. For rubella, there were 57,000 cases reported. For child molestation, those numbers of reported and confirmed molestations are only the tip of the iceberg. For every case reported there are at least two and maybe three more cases that never get reported.

That's why we may never know the exact number of child victims. We do know that if we use the conservative estimate that two in every ten little girls and one in every ten little boys are victims (based on the population reported in the 1999 U.S. Census statistical abstract) well over three million children are victims.

Take a moment to think about that. Three million children is a staggering number of children. *That's 46 National Football League stadiums packed with children who are, today, being sexually abused, and who believe they have no adult to go to for help.*

How Severe is the Damage?

Some people will say that sexually touching a child does no harm. Some adults will even tell boy victims to "act like a man" and "stop whining." Other adults are unsympathetic about the experiences of adult survivors. They will say that, no matter what happened in childhood, that is the past. You're an adult now, so get over it.

The facts are that sexual abuse does harm the child and that the damage often carries over into the child's adult life.

Studies show that this damage can include:

- difficulty in forming long-term relationships;
- sexual risk-taking that may lead to contracting sexually transmitted diseases, including AIDS;
- physical complaints and physical symptoms;
- depression, suicidal thoughts, and suicide;
- links to failure of the immune system and to increases in illnesses, hospitalizations, and early deaths.

In addition to the tangible physical and emotional damage that sexual abuse does to the child, that terrible secret that is held so close by two or three family members can go on to tear at the fiber of the family in generation after generation.

TABLE 2

Contrasts: Admitted Molesters vs. All American Men

	Admitted Child Molesters	American Men
Married or formerly married	77%	73%
Some College	46%	49%
High School only	30%	32%
Working	69%	64%
Religious	93%	93%

Sources: The Abel and Harlow Child Molestation Prevention Study and the 1999 U.S. Census Statistical Abstract

Note: All people in both groups were at least 25 years old.

Examining The Facts With Care

Is it possible that the profile of the child molester is this: a man who is married, educated, working, and religious?

Yes. However, we all have to be careful at this point. We have to ask the next question: What does this mean? To answer that we come to another finding from the Abel and Harlow Child Molestation Prevention Study.

Rather than *causing* a person to molest, being married, educated, working, and religious is who we are as Americans. These are the facts. It's crucial that everyone understands them. In order for adult protectors to stand as a barrier between their children and a child sexual abuser, the protectors have to know what a sexual abuser of children looks like. *He looks like George.*

And he looks like a lot of other people you know. In analyzing the reports of the 4,000 admitted child molesters researchers found this: in their outward characteristics, matching percentages of child molesters to percentages of all American men, *the average child molester closely matched the average American man.*

They matched all the outward characteristics listed in Table 2.

Which Ethnic Groups Molest Children?

Are there ethnic groups in which child molestation does not occur? Probably not. Results from the Abel and Harlow Child Molestation Prevention Study suggest that each ethnic group studied has child molesters among them. Once again, the percentages bear a resemblance to the U.S. Census. (See <u>The Abel and Harlow Child Molestation Prevention Study</u>" for further details about ethnic groups).

TABLE 3

Ethnic Groups: Admitted Molesters vs. All American Men

	Admitted Child Molesters	American Men
Caucasian	79%	72%
Hispanic/Latin-American	9%	11%
African-American	6%	12%
Asian	1%	4%
Native American	3%	1%

Sources: The Abel and Harlow Child Molestation Prevention Study and the 1999 U.S. Census Statistical Abstract

Note: 3,952 men who admitted to molesting children were compared to American men of various ethnic groups. Asians were under-represented in the complete sample of 15,508 men. They were 1.2 percent. Native Americans were over-represented in the complete sample. They were 3 percent. Both groups had child molesters in proportions equal to their percentages of representation in the complete sample.

Which Children Are Molested?

Children are most at risk from the adults in their own family, *and* from the adults who are in their parents' social circle. In fact, 90 percent of abusers target children in their own families and children who they know well. Furthermore, research suggests that the risk is across the board: Child molesters come from every part of our society, and so children from every part of our society are at risk.

TABLE 4

Which Children Do Child Molesters Target?

CHILDREN IN THE FAMILY	
Biological Child	19%
Stepchild, Adopted or Foster Child	30%
Brothers & Sisters	12%
Nieces & Nephews	18%
Grandchild	5%
CHILDREN IN THE NEIGHBORHOOD	
Child Left in My Care	5%
Child of Friend or Neighbor	40%
CHILDREN WHO ARE STRANGERS	
Child Strangers	10%

Source: The Abel and Harlow Child Molestation Prevention Study.

Note: Since sexual abusers of children often molest children in more than one category, the categories total more than 100 percent. The same child molester may have molested his biological child and his stepchild, therefore, we cannot say that those two categories combined represent 49 percent, but must say that they represent a lower number.

Notice that only 10 percent of the child sexual abusers report that they molest a child who is a stranger.

Let's put the facts together:

- Child molesters exist in every part of our society.
- They molest children close to them, mainly children in their family or children in their social circle.
- Most child molesters, 90 percent, report that they know their child victims very well.

We want you to look carefully at that last fact on the list. While there are several facts that you will use as part of The Child Molestation Prevention Plan, this is the most important.

To save the greatest number of children in the shortest possible time, we must turn the current focus of our efforts upside down. Right now, 90 percent of our efforts go toward protecting our children from strangers, when what we need to do is to focus 90 percent of our efforts toward protecting children from the abusers who are not strangers - the molesters in their families and the molesters who are the friends of their families.

And we must ask the next important question: What causes the one member of the family who molests to be so different from the rest of his or her family? To end nearly all child molestation we must focus on the cause.

Back to <u>2. Focus on the cause: An ongoing sex drive directed toward children.</u>

Warning Signs of Suicide

American Foundation *for* Suicide Prevention

Used by permission

Suicide can be prevented. While some suicides occur without any outward warning, most people who are suicidal do give warnings. Prevent the suicide of loved ones by learning to recognize the signs of someone at risk, taking those signs seriously and knowing how to respo9nd to them.:

- Observable signs of serious depression:
   Unrelenting low mood
   Pessimism
   Hopelessness
   Desperation
   Anxiety, psychic pain and inner tension
   Withdrawal
   Sleep problems
- Increased alcohol and/or other drug use
- Recent impulsiveness and taking unnecessary risks
- Threatening suicide or expressing a strong wish to die

- Making a plan:

    Giving away prized possessions

    Sudden or impulsive purchase of a firearm

    Obtaining other means of killing oneself such as poisons or medications
- Unexpected rage or anger

The emotional crises that usually precede suicide are often recognizable and treatable. Although most depressed people are not suicidal, most suicidal people are depressed. Serious depression can be manifested in obvious sadness, but often it is rather expressed as a loss of pleasure or withdrawal from activities that had been enjoyable. One can help prevent suicide through early recognition and treatment of depression and other psychiatric illnesses.

Resource Page

Southern California & Nationwide
Alphabetical Order
Organization and contacts
Used by permission

Please Support Any Of The Following 501c3 Organizations!

American Foundation for Suicide Prevention (AFSP) **is** ...the leading national not-for-profit organization exclusively dedicated to understanding and preventing suicide through research, education and advocacy, and to reaching out to people with mental disorders and those impacted by suicide.

Name of organization: American Foundation *for* Suicide Prevention

Phone number: 1-888-333-AFSP (2377)

Address: 120 Wall Street, 22nd Floor, New York, NY 10005

Website: www.afsp.org

Cedars Cultural and Educational Foundation- Los Angeles Preventing Abuse Conference is... advocating and fulfilling our civic responsibilities according to the biblical world view, in doing so:

1. We publish public policy statements on a wide variety of subjects from the moral issues to foreign policy.

2. Most predominantly we are deeply engaged in dealing with the problem of human trafficking, child abduction and internet

safety by holding conferences that focus to educate motivate and activate the public to be a part of the solution.

Name of organization: Cedars Cultural and Educational Foundation

Founders Name: Tony Nassif

Phone 818-848-7522

Address: P.O. Box 2851, Toluca Lake, CA. 91610

Website: www.cedarsfoundation.org and www.preventingabuse.org

---

The Child Molestation Research & Prevention Institute (CMRPI) is a national, science-based, 501(c)3, nonprofit organization with offices in Atlanta, GA and Oakland, CA. CMRPI conducts research to prevent child sexual abuse and provides information to prevention organizations, agencies, professionals, and families to use to prevent abuse.

1. To focus our scientific research on the major causes of child sexual abuse, especially in areas where early intervention can save the greatest number of children.

2. To provide scientific information that supports the prevention actions of the field, especially prevention organizations, professionals, and families.

Name of organization: Child Molestation Research & Prevention Institute

Founders Name: N/A

Phone number: (510) 808-0386

Address: 274 14th Street, Oakland, CA 94612

Website: http://www.childmolestationprevention.org/pages/about.html#contact_us

Or

Name of organization: Child Molestation Research & Prevention Institute

Phone: (404)872-5152

Address: 1401 Peachtree Street, Suite 120 Atlanta, GA 30309

Website: http://www.childmolestationprevention.org/pages/about.html#contact_us

Please note that we are not able to respond immediately and our response time varies. If you need more immediate assistance, we suggest you contact the Stop It Now! helpline at 1-888-PREVENT. You may also find other helpful resources under the "Resources" section of our website.

DAP is... "A Christian-based drug and alcohol treatment program with long term residency."

Name of organization: Drug Alternative Program

Founders Name: Cliff and Freddie Harris

Phone number: 909-783-1094

Address: 11868 Arliss Drive, Grand Terrace, Ca. 92313.

Website: www.drugalternativeprogram.com

Vivionne Keli is a member of the Community Coalition and supports this 501c3 organization

Door of Hope is... a "transitional housing for homeless families with children."

1. Our comprehensive supportive services include case management, counseling, life skills classes in budget/finance, parenting, marriage, Bible study, support groups, permanent housing placement, follow up care, and a holistic after school program M-F.

2. Our purpose is "to equip homeless families to rebuild their lives." This has been accomplished in over 220 families like Teresa who stayed at Door of Hope for 8 months with her 3 children after leaving a domestic violence situation and is now working full time at a local hospital and raising her children in safe permanent affordable housing.

3. Our goal is to break the cycle of homelessness through individualized plans for every family bringing hope and a future for generations to come.

Name of organization: Door of Hope

Founders Name: Steve Lazarian Sr.

Phone number: 626-304-9130

Address: Mailing P.O. Box 90455, Pasadena CA 91109

Website: www.doorofhope.us

Vivionne Keli works with this 501c3 organization

Downtown Women's Center is... is a provider of permanent supportive housing and a safe and healthy community fostering dignity, respect, and personal stability, and to advocate ending homelessness for women.

1. Founded in 1978, DWC remains the ***only*** organization on downtown Los Angeles' Skid Row singularly dedicated to serving the unique needs of homeless women.

2. A drop-in Day Center provides meals, case management, health services, and educational, employment, and enrichment programming for homeless and extremely low-income women as well as outreach to *survivors of human trafficking*.

3. Our adjacent residence provides permanent supportive housing for formerly homeless women.

Name of organization: Downtown Women's Center (DWC)

Founders Name: Jill Halverson

Phone number: 213-680-0600

Address: 325 S. Los Angeles Street, Los Angeles, CA 90013

Website: www.DWCweb.org

Vivionne Keli works with this 501c3 organization and has sat on their Board

End Times **Like These Ministries Inc. is**... a Social Services Ministry

1. Our Mission is to proclaim the Three Angels' Message; sharing the light of the gospel with others by meeting the immediate needs of the community conducting health seminars, evangelistic crusades and prophecy seminars.

2. We are a non-profit LAY MINISTRY, passionate about encouraging, educating, equipping and empowering other LAITY for soul winning, also deploying the trained into various fields to spread the gospel of Jesus Christ. In addition, our mission is to provide tools, information and training to churches so that each church can become an evangelistic center serving their communities year-round.

3. We are a Serve to Save Social Services Ministry that administers and fulfills the physical, mental and emotional needs of humanity by providing, Motel vouchers, Shelter referrals, Low income housing, Food, Clothing, Addiction assistance, Assistance for low income families, Employment assistance, Alternative Education referrals for troubled youth. Childcare referrals for single and low income parents. Ex-offender job and housing referrals, Personal and Family counseling and Drug Alternative Counseling.

Name of organization: End Times Like These Ministries Inc. **Serve to Save Social Services**

Founders Name: Michael & Denise Johnson

Phone: (805) 531-9718

Fax: (805) 531-9535

Address: P.O Box 426, Moorpark California 93020

Email: endtimes144@aol.com

Website: www.endtimeslikethese.org

Vivionne Keli works with this 501c3 organization with Giji Galang

Kids For Peace USA is... "cultivating every child's innate ability to foster peace through cross-cultural experiences and hands-on arts, service and environmental projects."

Name of organization: Kids For Peace USA

Founders Name: Danielle Gram and Jill McManigal

Phone number: (760) 730-3320

Address: Kids for Peace, 3303 James Drive,

Carlsbad, CA, 92008

Email: info@kidsforpeaceusa.org

Website: http://kidsforpeaceusa.org/

Vivionne Keli is a member of the Community Coalition and supports this 501c3 organization

Lake Avenue Community Foundation **is**.... a faith-based non-profit organization, unleashing the God-given potential of at-risk youth, providing the tools necessary to thrive academically, emotionally, economically, and spiritually.

1. Services: Tutoring, Mentoring, Homeless services including emergency aid and Healthcare services.

2. Our four key goals with neighborhood youth are: academic success – to help students excel academically and attend college; emotional health – to help students exhibit sound judgment, good problem-solving skills and meet daily challenges that aid in their success and emotional well being; economic stability – to help students become economically responsible and stable adults; and spiritual growth – to help students develop a thriving relationship with God.

3. This is being accomplished through our youth programs STARS (Students and Tutors Achieving Real Success) and Neighborhood Student Mentoring. In addition, Lake Avenue Community Foundation facilitates the Homeless and Community Outreach Program focusing on breaking the cycle of poverty and hopelessness while encouraging and equipping men and women in developing intimate relationships with God, the church and their families.

Name of organization: Lake Avenue Community Foundation

Board Chair: Bruce Stone,

Executive Director: John Wilson

Phone number: (626) 449-4960

Address: 712 E. Villa Street, Pasadena, CA 91101

Website: www.lakeavefoundation.org

The **Payne Family Foundation is**... Changing lives, one child at a time

1. Founded in 2007, the **Payne Family Foundation** was established as a 501(c) 3 public charity to develop effective partnerships with faith-based organizations, educational institutions, and community groups committed to ensuring that children and their families have access to the fundamental resources they need to live healthy and productive lives.

2. We provide resources and monetary grants to organizations that are committed to helping children and their families through medical care, educational/vocational programs, drug/crime prevention programs, employment training, parent-child relationship building, faith-based programs, life-skills training, and social/economic development.

Name of organization: Payne Family Foundation

Founder/Director: Dr. Pedro R. Payne

Phone number: (951) 992-9778

Address: P.O. Box 10125, Moreno Valley, CA. 92552

Website: www.paynefamilyfoundation.org

Resource Page

Vivionne Keli has supported POV in the past and completed their intervention training. To find out more about their intervention training please contact POV.

Peace Over Violence is... "A crisis intervention services to survivors of sexual and domestic."

1. We have a 24 Hour Rape & Battering Hotlines 626.793.3385 - 310.392.8381 - 213.626.3393. Through our 24 hour crisis line we offer emotional support, information & referrals.

2. We provide accompaniments to local law enforcement agencies and/or hospitals, advocacy, one on one counseling self-defense classes.

Name of organization: Peace Over Violence

Phone number: Tel: 213-955-9090

Fax: 213-955-9093

Address: 605 W Olympic Blvd Suite 400, Los Angeles CA 90015

Website: www.peaceoverviolence.org

Vivionne Keli is a member of the Community Coalition and supports this 501c3 organization

Stepping Stone is... "A provider of faith-based residential and supportive services for homeless and at-risk single mothers and their children, Stepping Stone mission is, *"Transforming the lives of single mothers and their children!"*

1. Stepping Stones for Women's mission is to transform the lives of single mothers and their children from cycles of hopelessness to the joy of faith and stability.

2. This is accomplished through housing, life skill development, mentoring, counseling, education, job rehabilitation and resources for long-term affordable housing.

3. One of Stepping Stones for Women's core values is the respect of each mother and child as a "diamond in the rough" that can be transformed through nurture and leadership.

Name of organization: Stepping Stones for Women

Founders Name: Wendy Fox & Stacy Gessinger

Executive Director: Kathy Benton

Phone number: 626-974-1162

Fax: 626-974-1984

Address: PO Box 4873, Covina, CA 91723

Website: www.ssfw.org

Resource Nationwide

The Hope of Survivors is... "A ministry of compassion providing support, hope and encouragement to victims of clergy sexual abuse and misconduct."

1. Reaching the Hurting...Ministering to those who have suffered abuse at the hands of clergy.

2. Calling the Faithful...Providing resources and support to church leadership to help them remain true to their high calling.

3. Bridging the Gap...Leading the hurting to hope through a healing relationship with Christ.

Name of organization: The Hope of Survivors Founders Name: Steve & Samantha Nelson

Phone number: (866) 260-8958

Address: P.O. Box 16, Thompsonville, IL 62890

Website: http://www.thehopeofsurvivors.com

Latino Division: La Esperanza de los Sobrevivientes

Website: http://www.laesperanzadelossobrevivientes.com

Women's Healing and Empowering Network... "W.H.E.Network helps to provide healing and empowerment to individuals, families, homes, churches, schools and other organizations through faith-based education, counseling, healing centers, resources and other support services in the areas of domestic violence, sexual abuse and related abuse.

We also assist religious organizations in establishing policies and procedures that will prevent child abuse, protect victims and hold perpetrators accountable for their actions."

Name of organization: W.H.E. Network

Founders Name: Dr. Mable Dunbar

Phone number: (509) 838-2761

Address: Women's Healing and Empowerment Network PO Box 19039 Spokane, WA 99219-9039

Website: http://www.whenetwork.org/

Verses on Promises NKJV

1. John 1:12 "But as many as received Him, to them He gave the *right **to become children of God**,* to those who believe in His name"

2. Colossians 2:9-10 "For in Him dwells all the fullness of the Godhead bodily; and **you are complete in Him**, who is the head of all principality and power."

3. 2 Corinthians 1:21-22 "Now He who *establishes us with you in Christ* and has anointed us *is* God,²² who also **has sealed us and given us the Spirit in our hearts as a guarantee**."

4. 2 Corinthians 5:17 "Therefore, if anyone *is* in Christ, **he is a new creation**; old things have passed away; behold, all things have become new."

5. James 1:5 "If any of you lacks wisdom, **let him *ask of God*, who gives to all** liberally and without reproach, and it will be given to him."

6. Hebrew 2:11 "For both He who sanctifies and those **who are being sanctified *are* all of one**, for which reason *He is not ashamed to call them brethren*

Verses on the Mind & Thoughts

1. Philippians 2:5-7 "Let this mind be in you which was also in Christ Jesus, who, being in the form of God, did not consider it robbery to be equal with God, but made Himself of no reputation, taking the form of a bondservant, and coming in the likeness of men.

2. 1 Chronicles 28:9 "As for you, my son Solomon, know the God of your father, and serve Him with a loyal heart and with a willing mind; for the LORD searches all hearts and understands all the intent of the thoughts. If you seek Him, He will be found by you; but if you forsake Him, He will cast you off forever."

3. Psalm 10:4 "The wicked in his proud countenance does not seek God; God is in none of his thoughts."

4. Psalm 40:5 "Many, O LORD my God, are Your wonderful works Which You have done; And Your thoughts toward us Cannot be recounted to You in order; If I would declare and speak of them, They are more than can be numbered."

5. Psalm 94:11 "The LORD knows the thoughts of man, That they are futile."

6. Psalm 139:17 "How precious also are Your thoughts to me, O God! How great is the sum of them!"

7. Proverbs 12:5 "The thoughts of the righteous are right, But the counsels of the wicked are deceitful."

8. Proverbs 15:26 "The thoughts of the wicked are an abomination to the LORD, But the words of the pure are pleasant."

9. Proverbs 16:3 "Commit your works to the LORD, And your thoughts will be established."

10. Isaiah 55:7 "Let the wicked forsake his way, And the unrighteous man his thoughts; Let him return to the LORD, And He will have mercy on him; And to our God, For He will abundantly pardon."

11. Isaiah 55:8 "For My thoughts are not your thoughts, Nor are your ways My ways," says the LORD."

12. Isaiah 65:2 "I have stretched out My hands all day long to a rebellious people, Who walk in a way that is not good, According to their own thoughts;"

13. Jeremiah 4:14 "O Jerusalem, wash your heart from wickedness, That you may be saved. How long shall your evil thoughts lodge within you?"

14. Jeremiah 6:19 "Hear, O earth! Behold, I will certainly bring calamity on this people— The fruit of their thoughts, Because they have not heeded My words Nor My law, but rejected it."

15. Leviticus 24:12 "Then they put him in custody, that the mind of the LORD might be shown to them."

16. Psalm 7:9 "Oh, let the wickedness of the wicked come to an end, But establish the just; For the righteous God tests the hearts and minds."

17. Psalm 26:2 "Examine me, O LORD, and prove me; Try my mind and my heart."

18. Philippians 2:1-4 "Therefore if there is any consolation in Christ, if any comfort of love, if any fellowship of the Spirit, if any affection and mercy, fulfill my joy by being like-minded, having the same love, being of one accord, of one mind. Let nothing be done through selfish ambition or conceit, but in lowliness of mind let each esteem others better than himself. Let each of you look out not only for his own interests, but also for the interests of others."

BIBLIOGRAPHY

Movies Mentioned

1. Sybil. Dir. Daniel Petrie. NBC Broadcast. 1976
2. Fatal Attraction. Dir. Adrian Lyne. Paramount Pictures. 1987
3. Mommie Dearest. Dir. Frank Perry. Paramount Pictures. 1981

Made in the USA
Monee, IL
13 February 2020